DRAW NEAR

HEBREWS
ON CHRISTIAN
WORSHIP

THE REV.
CHARLIE
HOLT

Bible Study Media

Draw Near: Hebrews on Christian Worship

© 2019 by The Rev. Charlie Holt

All rights reserved.

Published in Houston, Texas by Bible Study Media, Inc.

Cover and Interior design by Tommy Owen Design.

ISBN # 978-1-942243-26-7

Library of Congress Control Number: 2019901072

Printed in the United States of America

Table of Contents

Welcome

A SERMON TO THE BAPTIZED

The letter to the Hebrews is more appropriately called the sermon to the Hebrews. Its writer would be better termed a preacher. He writes, *"I appeal to you, brothers and sisters, bear with my word of exhortation, for I have written to you briefly"* (Hebrews 13:22). The act of exhortation has an aim of persuasion and motivation. So, what is the preacher of this sermon exhorting us to do? He is challenging us to worship, pure and simple. The book of Hebrews is an exhortation to a deep, abiding worship of the Living God, in and through Jesus Christ.

The sermon is written to all baptized Christians. The exhortation is to go deeper and become more intimate with the Living God. The preacher's concern is that the pain and trials common to Christians who live in a fallen world would tempt faithful members to shrink back from a vibrant faith and warm communion with the Living God. The antidote to falling away is drawing near.

Not only is the letter to the Hebrews to be read and contemplated as a sermon delivered within the context of a Christian worship service, but also it is primarily a sermon *about the context of Christian worship*. More than any other book of the New Testament, the sermon teaches, encourages, and challenges the Christian to worship in the form and way the Living God desires.

For us, as followers of Christ in the twenty-first century, the challenge of this exhortation could not be more relevant. You and I live in a day when the baptized have become complacent in their relationship with God. Many have fallen out of the habit of regular participation in the corporate assemblies of the church. Worship attendance has fallen in the developed world to all-time lows.

On average, only 17.7% of the U.S. population is worshiping the Lord in the context of a Christian church on any given Sunday. [1] The typical church membership rolls are double the average Sunday attendance—only half of baptized church members are engaged in worship on the Lord's Day.

As I've discussed these trends with pastors of various denominations nationally, I've learned that it has become the norm—

"According to the Hartford Institute of Religion Research, more than 40 percent of people say they go to church every week, but statistics show that fewer than 20 percent actually attend. More than 4,000 churches close their doors every year. Between 2010 and 2012, half of all churches in the U.S. did not add any new members. Each year 2.7 million church members fall into inactivity."[2]

pastors around the country are seeing their congregations worship the Lord in community much less frequently than once a week. The drift is moving from every other week to once a month to once a quarter to twice a year. I have heard more than one pastor say, "My congregation is a different group of people every Sunday." The sad reality is that the hearts of the people of God are growing hard to the Word of the Lord. Zeal for the Lord is waning. It is to this very crisis of a lack of zeal that the sermon to the Hebrews speaks.

Let us hear again, the brief word of exhortation of the preacher: Be encouraged to fall in love with God in a deeper way. Pay attention, draw near, go deeper. Worship the Lord in the beauty of his holiness. We are being invited, indeed challenged, to enter in and come closer to the Living God through his Son, Jesus Christ.

I am faithfully yours in Christ Jesus our Lord,

Charlie Holt

[1] See David Olsen, The American Church in Crisis, (Grand Rapids, Zondervan, 2008) p. 28.
[2] Toni Ridgeway, "Statistics Don't Tell the Whole Story When It Comes to Church Attendance", churchleaders.com, October 7, 2013.

Introduction

HOW TO WORSHIP GOD

The Lord would have us be in an intimate relationship with him. God desires to be in communion with his people. Through that communion alone, we become a people that manifest a holy perfection and maturity. There are several beloved verses in the book of Hebrews that are often quoted and memorized, "*For the word of God is living and active, sharper than any two-edged sword*" (4:12) and "*Now faith is the assurance of things hoped for, the conviction of things not seen*" (11:1). For all the beautiful memory verses on faith and grace, these themes are minor notes that serve to underscore the major melody line: worship. To be even clearer, Hebrews is about how to worship the Living God in a new and living way that has never been open to the people of this planet until now. Since the resurrection of Christ and the rending of the temple veil, we are invited to approach the throne of the High King of Heaven directly! How do we accept such a privilege? We begin with a heart of praise, as the well-known hymn captures:

> *Praise, my soul, the King of Heaven;*
> *To His feet thy tribute bring.*
> *Ransomed, healed, restored, forgiven,*
> *Evermore His praises sing:*
> *Alleluia!, Alleluia!*
> *Praise the everlasting King.* [3]

A Christian worship service is an approach to the throne of the High King of Heaven. How do you worship the King of Heaven? Is there a proper way to approach the everlasting King? *To his feet, thy tribute bring.*

As a young Christian, I used to think that the more formal, liturgical churches were following a corrupt and dead tradition while the more contemporary churches were alive and true to the Bible. To me, even the word "liturgy" implied boring and spiritually dead. Admittedly,

---

[3] Praise my soul, the King of Heaven. By Henry Francis Lyte (1834). Music by John Goss (1869).

personal experience and some bad teaching had shaped my perspective. I remember the chapel services held in the school cafeteria at my Episcopal high school. One of our priests suffered from narcolepsy. He was constantly falling asleep during the other priest's sermons. If the priests themselves were falling asleep, the services had to be dull!

Worship as it is described in the Bible is anything but boring. The preacher of Hebrews describes the approach into the Lord's presence as absolutely awesome—*"our God is a consuming fire"* (12:29). Yet something has happened in Christian worship in the 21st century that has prevented us from experiencing God in such a powerful way.

I suggest that it has to do directly with a lack of knowledge and misunderstanding of New Testament books of the Bible which provide encouragements and instructions for worship, particularly the book of Hebrews. First, we have not understood that the book of Hebrews and its exhortations are to be read and applied *within the context of worship*—a worship service is the soil where the seeds of Hebrews' deep teaching will grow. Second, we have forgotten that the exhortation of Hebrews teaches us *how to worship*.

The Bible in the Context of Worship

The writer of Hebrews describes his letter as an exhortation—a sermon. It is intended to speak into the context of a worshiping community. Even when it is studied without consideration of a community in worship, it remains instructive; however, it does not reach its fullest potential as a sermon intended to inspire zealous and faithful worship. For example, one could study a bicycle and all its various parts in a bike shop. You could learn the mechanics of it—how the chain, spokes, wheels, and handlebars are all designed and fit together. However, the only way to truly understand how a bike functions is to use it, to experience it, take it out on the road for a spin.

As you progress through your study of Hebrews, allow its exhortation to translate directly to the practicalities of your worship of God in and through Jesus Christ. Take what you read and discuss in your group and apply it directly to the practice of your worship community on Sunday morning. Through your study of his Word, God is calling you into a deeper relationship with himself. Open your eyes and soften your heart to his love. Apply what you learn from his Word to active worship.

The book of Hebrews, then, is written to lead us into a deeper intimacy with the Living God as we bring its words directly into the context of worship. This is a practice we must recover to fully experience its rich blessings. This leads to our second problem. We have forgotten not only the context within which to read this word of exhortation, but also the very heart of its teaching: Hebrews is a guide to *how we ought to worship*.

Worship in the Context of the Bible

We have lost the shape and structure of biblical Christian worship. If there is one thing that we should learn from the study of the Bible as a whole, it is that God determines and sets the terms of our relationship with him. He is God; we are not. In the days of the Old Covenant, worshipers were given very specific instructions about how God was to be approached in worship. With the advent of the New Covenant in Jesus Christ, this fact has not changed. Worshipers are still given very specific instructions on how God is to be approached in worship.

We still approach the Lord on his terms—in his way. As such, it is important to remember that the liturgies of the Christian tradition reflect a consistent pattern that is derived directly from the Bible. Unfortunately, the church has largely forgotten this. In far too many congregations, the clergy and people of God simply go through the liturgical motions without a lot of understanding or thought as to why they are doing what they are doing. The result is a gathering with very little power or effect in the lives of those participating. Church becomes boring and lifeless.

Much of what passes as traditional worship is like a lifeless skeleton, without flesh and muscle—mere bones.

This sad reality has led to a dangerous overreaction. The contemporary church has jettisoned much of the form and pattern of the traditional worship service in search of a more "authentic" and powerful experience with God. Yet, these modern-day worship services often lack biblical structure and direction as well as spiritual intention.

The contemporary church service is often a spectator event where those on the stage are entertaining a relatively passive audience. Such worship services can be powerful and exciting *to watch and hear*. However, do they really accomplish what the Bible is calling us to in a worship service? Is there an active participation and communion with the Living God that is lacking? In a way, it is the opposite of a skeleton-like liturgy without flesh and muscle—it is a body without bones, a blob of flesh and muscle, lacking structural support.

Sadly, the critique of traditional liturgy that has led to a largely formless contemporary church service is warranted, not because the forms themselves are lacking, but rather because the church has by-and-large forgotten the basis for the liturgical forms and how they are supposed to be used. The problems have been compounded by denominational divisions. The church tends to cluster around denominational distinctions such as the Charismatic/Pentecostal, the Evangelical, and the Liturgical (catholic/universal.) The catholic liturgical forms only gain their dynamism when the evangelical Word of God is preached and the charisma of the Holy Spirit indwells the people of God.

There is a biblical pattern and structure to worshiping God that is both bones (structure) and flesh (life). The book of Hebrews shows us the way. The book begins with communication about our need to be attentive to the Word of God as it speaks to us (Chapters 1-4), but it leads to a consummation of the relationship between the Savior and us in the sacramental experience of spiritually partaking by faith his body and blood (Chapters 5-10). The final chapters charge us to live the life of acceptable worship boldly and bodily, in the world, by faith (Chapters 11-13).

Jesus is both the *way in* and the *way out* of the holy sanctuary of God's spiritual presence. Jesus is the one speaking to us by his powerful Word, which is sharper than any two-edged sword. As the one ministering to us as the Great High Priest, Jesus ushers us behind the curtain of the Holy of Holies. He partook in the weakness of our humanity that we might partake in his divine nature. He tasted death for us that we might taste new life in him. He is the lamb upon the altar, the great sacrifice for sin that was performed outside the camp. The location of the sacrifice, taking place outside the sanctuary, symbolizes our call to witness to Christ's love both to people who are inside the camp (other believers) and to those outside, even those who may be hostile to him though desperately in need of his grace.

The movement in a worship service is first *in* and then *out*. We are called and drawn in to a place of intimacy with the Living God that we may then be sent out in powerful witness to him. The exhortations in Hebrews move us from the one place to the other. We are exhorted to *"pay greater attention"* (2:1) to what we have heard in the Word, allowing it to pierce our hearts in conviction like a sharp *"two-edged sword"* (4:12). Then we may *"draw near to the throne of grace"* (4:16) so that we *"enter the sanctuary by the blood of Jesus, by the new and living way that he opened for us through the curtain (that is, through his flesh)"* (10:19-20). Finally, we are sent out into the world in witness to his love, commissioned and empowered to live in the world, by faith, as living sacrifices that *"go to him outside the camp and bear the abuse he endured"* (13:13).

Having our attention captivated to our core, we are called to draw near to the throne room of grace. There the Great High Priest will minister to us by his sacrifice of himself, offered once for all, and through his perpetual intercession for us at the throne, the most holy place—heavenly Mount Zion.

Having made our approach to the holy mountain of God in awesome worship, we will follow Jesus from the sanctuary out into the world to both suffer with him, when called, and to testify to his love and power. But first, let us *draw near*.

Week 1

ATTENDING TO THE WORD OF THE LORD

Therefore, we must pay much closer attention to what we have heard, lest we drift away from it. For since the message declared by angels proved to be reliable, and every transgression or disobedience received a just retribution, how shall we escape if we neglect such a great salvation?

HEBREWS 2:1-3A

Day 1

Christian worship begins with an assumption—God is there and he is not silent. God has spoken. Indeed, God is speaking. We are privileged to listen.

God has spoken in the past in various ways through his prophets. We hear their words every time we read a passage from the Old Testament. I have often thought how wonderful it will be to someday meet Moses or Abraham in the heavenly realms and ask, "What was it like to experience God in such powerful ways?"

Wouldn't you love to hear Abraham personally tell the story of receiving God's covenant and watching the blazing torch pass between the sacrifices? Or Moses describe the moment he heard the Lord's voice speaking from a bush on fire? God revealed himself to men like Abraham, Moses, Elijah, and other prophets in mighty ways. We marvel at the signs and wonders he used to speak to and through them.

This may surprise you, but the prophets and leaders of the Old Testament who are in heaven will one day be more eager to hear of our experiences than to share theirs. That's because the revelation of God to us and the way in which he speaks to us now far surpass the experience of those in the Old Testament.

How can this be? How could our experience be greater than the fiery pillars? More powerful than smoking mountains? Because we have the word of God himself, the Son of God, speaking to us! The people of old heard God's voice mediated by angelic messengers and prophets. We hear God's voice directly and in fullness through the Son.

> *Long ago God spoke to our ancestors in many and various ways*
> *by the prophets, but in these last days he has spoken to us by a*

Son whom he appointed heir of all things, through whom he also created the worlds. He is the reflection of God's glory and the exact imprint of God's very being, and he sustains all things by his powerful word. When he had made purification for sins, he sat down at the right hand of the Majesty on high, having become as much superior to angels as the name he has inherited is more excellent than theirs.

HEBREWS 1:1-4

Christian worship, then, begins with the assumption that God speaks, both powerfully and intimately. But what is the aim of worship?

The aim of Christian worship is to *bless God*.

This, too, may be surprising. In modern worship settings, the service often begins with a greeting to the gatherers: "Good morning, everyone, and welcome!" Contrary to this practice, the opening acclamation in a liturgical church aims to bless God: "Blessed be God: Father, Son and Holy Spirit. And blessed be his kingdom, now and forever" (BCP, p. 355). This blessing of God comes before any greeting of the people gathered: "The Lord be with you, and also with you."

The tradition of divine liturgy aims to bless and proclaim the triune God as the foremost starting point. The vertical relationship is primary, and the horizontal relationships are secondary. The reversal of this form in contemporary worship comes from a misconception of what worship is—the misunderstanding is that we enter worship *to be blessed*. This is exactly backwards. We *bless God* first, and in so doing, are blessed by him in return.

The reason a human-centered focus has become the norm is because many seeker-sensitive services assume people are starting from a position of doubt and need to be moved toward a position of belief. But this assumption leads into a prison of self-centeredness. If we begin from a point of "doubt of the divine," we are focusing the service on ourselves and our states of mind and heart. These become preeminent, rather than God.

But the basic premise of the Bible is that the starting place for all effective human reasoning is not doubt, but *faith* in the Living God. Human knowledge and wisdom begin with the recognition of a God who reveals himself. Solomon, considered the wisest of men, equates the starting place of knowledge with reverence for the Lord: "*The fear of the Lord is the beginning of knowledge*" (Proverbs 1:7a).

So, if we begin worship not with the assumption of doubt, but with the acknowledgement of a *God who speaks*—speaks his precious and great promises to us through his Son—our focus becomes God and his invitation to us to become partakers of the divine nature (2 Peter 1:4).

The shift in starting point is subtle, but it makes all the difference both in worship and in our lives. We can worship by focusing on ourselves in an effort to be blessed, or we can worship by blessing God and receive his blessing in response. We can lead either a self-centered life that results in discontentment and despair, or we can lead a God-centered life that results in peace and joy, even in times of great pain. But we will never get out of ourselves or beyond our self-focus until God's revelation to us becomes our starting point in both worship and life. Interestingly, this God-centered focus is what actually moves the human heart from doubt to belief, if only we would trust the process.

> *His divine power has granted to us all things that pertain to life and godliness, through the knowledge of him who called us to his own glory and excellence, by which he has granted to us his precious and very great promises, so that through them you may become partakers of the divine nature, having escaped from the corruption that is in the world because of sinful desire.*

2 PETER 1:3-4

The liturgies of traditional worship have always assumed a two-part experience: divine revelation (what we've been talking about) and human response. What then is our human response in worship?

Reflection:

"O Lord, open my lips, and my mouth will declare your praise." (Psalm 51:15).
Aware of our sins and shortcomings, we as penitent worshipers
understand that unless God opens our mouths, what comes out will be
something other than God-glorifying. Yet we are assured that if we ask
God to open our lips, pure praise will rise. So we ask God to open our
lips in praise—a declaration of praise to *God* that begins with *God*. Our
praise requires empowerment from him. Would you say that you have
been living a God-glorifying or a self-glorifying life recently, and why?
What could happen to your daily orientation if your first spoken sentence
was Psalm 51:15: *"O Lord, open my lips, and my mouth will declare your praise"*?

COGITO, ERGO SUM

In the days of the Enlightenment, a philosopher named René Descartes coined a now famous phrase, *"Cogito, ergo sum."* (Latin: "I think, therefore I am.") In very simplistic terms, he was wrestling with the philosophical problem of human consciousness. Until then, most people embraced basic truths about the existence of God and themselves. However, Enlightenment philosophers like Descartes called everything into question in a relentless search for certainty. In his *Meditations on First Philosophy*, Descartes wrote, "If you would be a real seeker after truth, it is necessary that at least once in your life you doubt, as far as possible, all things."

Descartes filled his mind with doubts about God, revelation, knowledge, even his own existence. Yet the "certainties" he found were in continual flux. He said of God, "…I have long had fixed in my mind the belief that an all-powerful God existed by whom I have been created such as I am." But later he postulated that perhaps an evil demon had deceived him into this original certainty: "I shall then suppose, not that God who is supremely good and the fountain of truth, but some evil genius not less powerful than deceitful, has employed his whole energies in deceiving me; I shall consider that the heavens, the earth, colors, figures, sound, and all other external things are nought but the illusions and dreams of which this genius has availed himself in order to lay traps for my credulity…". Descartes contemplated virtual reality before there was virtual reality!

There have been several dystopian movies in our day that postulate the same idea—that life is unknowable and potentially all illusion—one of the more famous being *The Matrix*. Morpheus, a character in the film, asks, "What is real? How do you define real? If you're talking about what you can feel, what you can smell, what you can taste and see, then real is simply electrical signals interpreted by your brain."

He continues: "Have you ever had a dream, Neo, that seemed so sure it was real? But if you were unable to wake up from that dream, how would you tell the difference between the dream world and the real world?"

Nearly 400 years before *The Matrix*, Descartes' personal breakthrough was to conclude that because he was aware of his own thought, he must exist: "I think, therefore I am." Human self-awareness became the launching point of modern philosophy and Descartes' line of reasoning emerged as one of the philosophical bases of the modern era. We have been working from his basic premise ever since—that man is the measure of all things—without giving it a second thought.

Consider that Descartes did not question his own decision to doubt everything as the starting point for knowledge. Could it be that his embrace of doubt was the invitation to "the evil demon?" Was it not Satan who introduced to humanity the question, "Did God really say?"

Our culture has whole-heartedly embraced this acceptance of doubt as the path to knowledge. We doubt God. But notice, we do not doubt ourselves. As a result, we are trapped in our own godless and self-centered thoughts. The consequence of this shift from faith-centeredness to doubt-centeredness is grave—we are violent, corrupt, driven by passions and lusts; we have become de-humanized.

Day 2

In Greek mythology, Narcissus was a young hunter blessed with amazing beauty. One day he came upon a reflective pool, gazed into it, and was captivated by his own reflection. He found himself unable to look away, despite the loving calls of a young woman named Echo. The tragedy of Narcissus is that he missed out on true love by choosing instead to focus on himself and his own self-love.

God is calling for our us, like the young Echo. He wants our attention. But in our culture of media and electronic devices that are constantly reflecting our self-images back to us in such captivating ways, we too become lost in a narcissistic gaze. We tune out the word of the Lord speaking to us—it becomes merely a distant echo. We also fail to recognize, like Narcissus, that the medium itself is powerful—it draws us in, promising us meaning and contentment it will never deliver. Narcissus withered away and died still staring at himself, never realizing that real love could never be found within the pool, only beyond it.

The Medium is the Message

In the opening chapter of his book *Understanding Media: The Extensions of Man*, Marshall McLuhan coined the phrase, "The medium is the message." Reading his opening chapter, you get a sense of his frustration with his contemporaries who had all but ignored the various new media through which content reached consumers, particularly television.

McLuhan's point is that a failure to recognize the power of a particular media itself, apart from its message, is naïve and dangerous.

For any medium has the power of imposing its own assumption on the unwary. We must use prediction and control to avoid the subliminal state of a Narcissus trance. But the greatest aid to this end is simply in knowing that the spell can occur immediately upon contact.

In this digital age, we are captivated by the content delivered to us by the latest computer, smart phone, tablet, or television. We tend to focus exclusively on the content and miss the fact that the screen itself is a kind of "message" we are falling for—it has us in its hold. More than fifty years after McLuhan's observation, we now know that various media not only influence our brains, but actually reshape them.

In Christian liturgy, there is also "media" and "message," or form and content. We receive the "message" of the Gospel through the "media" of the liturgy. And, in the same way that the electronic media we engage with shapes us, so liturgy itself influences us. The difference is that liturgy is designed to influence us toward God, not away from him. Liturgical forms actually put our hearts, minds, and bodies in a place where we can best receive the message of the word of God. For example, when we kneel for communion, the kneeling down itself conveys to our hearts and minds a sense of humility (kneeling is a humble position, usually reserved for a subject of royalty) and this humility reinforces the message that we have been welcomed to approach the presence of the Living God, humbly yet confidently.

This is why it is important that we take seriously not only the content of Christian worship (i.e., the word), but also the sacramental media through which that word is delivered. The forms of the liturgy themselves are powerfully shaping us as much as the content they deliver. This has long been recognized by the Church in the Latin maxim, "*Lex orandi, lex credendi*" which is literally translated, "The law of prayer is the law of belief." In this instance, prayer refers to the whole service of worship—an ongoing prayer in various forms. The way we worship and pray forms what and how we believe. Simply put, praying shapes believing. The liturgy patterns our minds and ingrains our hearts and souls with the message. The forms themselves create deep tracks for the word of God to be powerfully delivered. The medium is the message.

Taking this truth into account, when we engage the content of the Scriptures and the sermon during worship, it is critically important to recognize that the lector and the preacher are agents of the Living God. The illuminating power of the Holy Spirit invisibly sheds light on the spoken word. The medium and the message are to be seen together. To put it another way, when we listen to the Scriptures being read, it is important to notice not only what is being said but *who* is saying it. Who is speaking is the essence of the "media" of the liturgy. In the liturgy of the Church, the *who* speaking is the living Lord Jesus Christ, and the *what* being spoken is the word and sacrament.

It is easy to come into a Christian worship service and focus merely on the content being delivered, so much so that we completely miss that we are interacting with Jesus. But notice that after the Scriptures are read by lectors (readers), there is an acknowledgement that *God has just spoken to us*. After each reading, the lector says, "The Word of the Lord" to which the congregation responds, "Thanks be to God." The message (the word) was delivered through the media (the Lord speaking). Here is where Christian imagination and faith must come to bear in the divine liturgy: God is speaking to us.

Above the Angels

What role does Jesus, the Son, play in the liturgy?

Angelic messengers from the Lord addressed the people of God through men like Moses and the prophets. They inspired awe and action to the people of old. Yet, they were mere servants to the divine Son of God. As people of the New Covenant, we are no longer hearing the message of angels mediated by prophets, but in these last days of redemptive history, we are now spoken to by the supreme voice of the Son. The Father never bestowed "sonship" on the angels. On the contrary, the angels are to ascribe worship to the Son and serve him as his ministers of wind and flame. The point cannot be emphasized more strongly. The pecking order in the divine creation showcases the divine-human Son of God at the pinnacle of creation, above the angels. While God could have manifested his supreme word as an angel, he decided to elevate humanity above the angels in the divine-human son.

As the divine Son of God, Jesus is both the *content* of the speech of God (the word) and, in Christian worship, the *means* through which the message about himself is delivered. We affirm the superiority of the Son over angelic messengers because Jesus is the second person of the triune God. He is God in the flesh, divinity, and humanity as one—two natures, one person. Jesus' word stands above all other prophetic words because the Son is over all creation. Of the Son he says, "*You Lord laid the foundation of the earth in the beginning*" (Hebrews 1:10).

The preacher of Hebrews calls us to listen to the voice of the King— Jesus, the King of the world. Jesus is the creator of the world, the Son of God, the sustainer of the universe. In a Christian service of worship, the King is addressing his people. Ask yourself: as you hear the Scriptures read in church, as you hear the word throughout the liturgy, are you listening not only to what is being said, but to the One who is saying it? Let us never forget that the liturgy of the word is actually a human interaction with the Son of God, the Lord and King of the Universe!

Reflection:

Notice that the preacher of Hebrews uses the term "God says…" before he quotes the Old Testament Scriptures. The Scriptures are the word of God. But the Scriptures are not a dead letter. They speak today as loudly and lively as when first penned. He will later call the word "living and active." When you approach the Scriptures, whether in devotional reading or in the setting of corporate worship, how do you prepare yourself to receive the voice of the Lord?

The title "Son of God" is understood to refer to Jesus' divinity as the second person of the Trinity: Father, Son, and Holy Spirit. However, in the Old Testament, the title is also used for the human king of Israel. Two critical texts in this regard are 2 Samuel 7 and Psalm 2.

In 2 Samuel 7, we find the establishment of God's eternal covenant with David and his offspring. The throne and kingdom of David are everlasting, by the promise of God. Three times the Lord repeats the promise that David's throne will be established forever. The key verse for the writer of Hebrews is 2 Samuel 7:14: *I will be to him a father, and he shall be a son to me.*

The Davidic king is called the Son of God. The declaration of sonship establishes the king of Israel as eternally beloved by the Lord and divinely authorized to rule…forever.

We find this again in Psalm 2. The psalm is most likely one that was used at kingly coronation ceremonies. Envision the Psalm being dramatically enacted by choirs and liturgists during the king's enthronement. It has 4 parts:

1. The nations' rebellious reaction to the rule of the Lord and the Messiah (verses 1-3)

2. The Lord's response (verses 4-6)

3. The king's response (verses 7-9)

4. A call for response by the kings and rulers of the World (verses 10-12)

In part three, the King rehearses his divine authorization to rule with these words:

> *The Lord said to me, "You are my Son;*
> *today I have begotten you.*
> *Ask of me, and I will make the nations your heritage,*
> *and the ends of the earth your possession."*

PSALM 2:7-8

Again, the divine authorization of the king of David's line as Son of God imbues him with divine authority, rule, and power. This title is a foreshadowing of the Son of God, Jesus, of the line of David, who *as a human* will rule on the throne of God for all eternity.

Day 3

In the age of mass communication, we are inundated with a myriad of messages. Social media, television, radio, songs, emails, texts, tweets, and posts bombard us daily, making a claim for our attention and our belief. Much of what we see, hear, and read is untrue, half true, or "fake news."

We are also the most cynical and the most gullible generation. How is that possible? Well, we deeply distrust traditional authorities, but we naturally want to trust *some* authority, so we become gullible to the claims of conspiracy theorists, false prophets, gurus, demagogues, and other alternative authorities.

This distrust of some authorities yet quick embrace of others has created a real crisis for the Church. How can a person discern the authenticity and validity of the message of salvation? Is it really true that God wants to be in a personal relationship with me? How can I know that he cares? Is the death of Jesus on a cross 2000 years ago relevant to me today?

The validation of any message stems from the confirmation of multiple reliable sources. With respect to the message of salvation, it is made valid by the testimony of four key witnesses: the Father's signs and wonders, the work of the Son, the Holy Spirit's gifts, and the Apostolic witness.

> *It was declared to us at first by the Lord, attested to us by those who heard, while God also bore witness by signs and wonders and various miracles and by the gifts of the Holy Spirit distributed according to his will.*

HEBREWS 2:3-4

Note that all three persons of the godhead have confirmed our salvation. The Father testified to it by miraculous signs; the Son enacted it by his words, miracles, and redemptive work; and the Holy Spirit attested to it by the distribution of gifts. Together, the Father, the Son, and the Holy

Spirit are calling us to themselves so that we might enter into the trinity of worship and the worship of the Trinity.

We also have the eyewitness testimony of multiple apostles who experienced first-hand the Lord Jesus' mighty work for us and his message of promise. Since then, we have the testimony of millions who have persuasively lived out their faith. When I was a new Christian, it was this last evidence that held the most weight for me. I encountered many people whose lives testified to their personal life-changing experience with Jesus' life, ministry, death, and resurrection.

The Message of Worship

In our worship service, we have four Scripture readings: an Old Testament, a Psalm, a New Testament epistle, and a Gospel. The readings are in reverse order of primacy as they build to a crescendo with the reading of the Gospel.

The Gospel book is taken to the center of the congregation by a deacon and elevated to prominence with these words, "The Holy Gospel of our Lord Jesus Christ" to which the congregation responds, "Glory to you, Lord Christ." With that liturgical action, the deacon and the congregation have just recognized that the Lord Jesus Christ is present and that he is about to address us. After the reading, we have a similar acknowledgement when the deacon says, "The Gospel of the Lord" with the response, "Praise to you, Lord Christ." The risen Lord Jesus Christ has just addressed his people.

The writer of Hebrews exhorts the people of the Church to be "attentive" and "responsive" to the liturgy of the word, for it is none other than the Son of God who is speaking to them from the throne of heaven. When you come into worship and hear the Scriptures read and the Gospel preached, recognize it as the Lord Jesus speaking to you. In the book of Revelation, the Apostle John sees the Lord Jesus walking among the lampstands of the churches and writes, "*Hear what the spirit is saying to the churches.*" As we gather in worship to hear the word of God spoken, the Lord Jesus walks among us. When we worship, we come into the presence of the King.

Pay Attention

The exhortation of Hebrews urges us to pay closer attention to what we have heard. If the stakes were high when the Lord spoke through the angels and prophets, how much higher are they when he speaks through the Son? In yesterday's reading, we focused on the messenger. Today we focus on the message. Not only do we need to be aware of *who* is speaking to us, Jesus Christ, but we also need to pay very close attention to *what* he is saying.

The content of the King's speech is centered on *"such a great salvation."* This great salvation is offered and attested to us by none other than the Triune God—Father, Son, and Holy Spirit. We are being called and invited into the great salvation of God from sin, evil, death, and hell.

When I was ordained to be a priest of the Church, my Bishop at the time questioned me as part of the ordination rite, "Will you be loyal to the doctrines, discipline, and worship of Christ as this Church has received them?" I answered, "I am willing and ready to do so; and I solemnly declare that I do believe the Holy Scriptures of the Old and New Testaments to be the word of God, and to contain all things necessary to salvation." The priest's ordination vow is a commitment to both the *who* and the *what*. The *who* is Jesus Christ. Concerning the *what*, the first belief is that the Scriptures are the word of God and the second is that the Scriptures provide the only sufficient answer to humanity's most fundamental need—salvation.

The King of the Universe is continually addressing his people. He has something to say to us every single week and warns us to continually listen. Stop listening to the King's voice and instruction, and you will drift.

Therefore we must pay much closer attention to what we have heard, lest we drift away from it. For since the message declared by angels proved to be reliable, and every transgression or disobedience received a just retribution, how shall we escape if we neglect such a great salvation?

HEBREWS 2:1-3

If we come into the presence of the King and ignore his word as it is preached, read, and taught, and if we fail to apply it to our lives and hearts, then we are neglecting our own salvation. I have seen it happen to far too many people. We flounder and fail in life because we neglect the most important things. You may have heard the saying, "Keep the main thing, the main thing." It is true.

As humans, we are far too easily distracted from the most important things in pursuit of the trivial and the unimportant. In business, we can become easily distracted by new technologies or the latest and greatest advertising strategy. But take focus off the core product or service of the business, and the bottom line will suffer. In marriage, neglect to love and listen to your spouse and it will not matter how successful you are at providing, home-making, or child-rearing.

The same goes for our relationship with God. By falling into inattentiveness to the word spoken by the word (the Son), the people of God neglect "such a great salvation" and invite a horrible consequence far graver than any experienced by those who rebelled against the angelic messengers.

The Primacy of Worship

Worshiping the Living God is the most important thing we will ever do as human beings. Nothing less than our salvation is at stake. But what is the most important thing to do within the context of worship? The preacher tells us: Pay attention to voice of Jesus offering a great salvation. (And what an awesome salvation it is!) Do not neglect such a great salvation, but pay attention to it as the supreme revelation of God's word.

When you walk into a worship service, you are walking into the presence of the Holy Trinity and the Kingdom of God. Worship is about bringing glory and honor to God, and that's what we're invited to do just by walking through the church doors and listening. It is a holy, holy, holy experience. As the word of God begins to pour forth from the lectern and from the word preached, be attentive to it. Allow the word to penetrate your heart and mind and to inform you. The Lord Jesus is addressing you. Trust the validity of his message as an attested and confirmed word—your Lord is offering a sure word of hope to your heart in the message of such a great salvation.

Reflection:

Do you ever find your attention drifting during worship? Maybe you walk in to the service with your eyes glued to your phone or you immediately begin to socialize? Reflect on some methods you can use to bring your attention back to the Lord and the worship in which you partake. How can you be a better listener?

Day 4

So let's focus more sharply on what the Scriptures mean by "*a great salvation.*" The goal of salvation is the exaltation of humanity.

> *What is man, that you are mindful of him,*
> *or the son of man, that you care for him?*
> *You made him for a little while lower than the angels;*
> *you have crowned him with glory and honor,*
> *putting everything in subjection under his feet.*

HEBREWS 2:6 (QUOTING PSALM 8:6-8)

What is man? Does humanity have some purpose or reason for existence? Are we as human beings significant to God? On the one hand, considering all the vastness of God's creation, one might understandably answer, "Not very." We are small and insignificant compared to the vast expanse of interstellar space.

Consider Psalm 8, authored by King David. It is the first praise psalm of the Psalter. The psalm begins and ends with exaltation of the name of God: "*O LORD, our Lord, how majestic is your name in all the earth!*" As the psalmist extols the glories of God and the magnificence of creation—the heavens, the moon, and the stars—he ponders existentially the position of humanity. Indeed, to consider the vastness of God and his universe is to conclude that humanity is quite small by comparison. Who are we, compared to so much? This is a perennial question. However, David reminds himself of the creation mandate.

The first chapter of Genesis teaches that the creation of humanity was the crowning achievement of God. In Genesis 1:27-28, we find the creation mandate for humanity:

So God created man in his own image,
in the image of God he created him;
male and female he created them.

And God blessed them. And God said to them, "Be fruitful and
multiply and fill the earth and subdue it, and have dominion over
the fish of the sea and over the birds of the heavens and over every
living thing that moves on the earth."

The creation mandate can be easily remembered as three R's: Reflect, Reproduce, and Rule. We were made to *reflect* God's glory as image bearers, *reproduce* that image by fruitful multiplication, and bring God's image to bear as the *rulers* of the created order.

With the fall of humanity, mankind was diminished in its rule over the creation. The Scriptures teach that we were subjected to angelic rule, protection, and guard. Angelic sentinels were dispatched to prevent us from accessing Eden (Genesis 3:24). David expresses this idea in Psalm 8: *"You have made [man] a little lower than the angels"* (Psalm 8:5, NIV). We have also become subjected to evil angelic control. Satan, a fallen angel, enlisted humanity through temptation and intimidation to fulfill the devil's will in the Garden of Eden. Today, Satan and his legions still subject humanity to the fear of death, enslaving us under their tyranny.

In light of this subjugation, the message of our "great salvation" is nothing less than the announcement of the end of the satanic reign of terror. With the coming of Jesus, humanity is liberated to its rightful status in fulfilling the creation mandate.

The diminutive *"a little"* in the original Hebrew version of Psalm 8 describes place, position, or status. Man was made *"a little lower than the angels,"* meaning that, in the pecking order of creation, we are just below the angels. A high position of importance and significance indeed! The preacher of Hebrews expands on the psalm and illuminates its truth in ways that King David may not have imagined. For example, the preacher zeroes in on the word *"a little"* and interprets it in a temporal sense rather than a positional one. Yes, there is a positional subjection of mankind under the angelic hosts, but we are made lower only for *"a little while."* Any subjection of humanity under the angelic realm (good or bad) is temporary in nature. For, as the psalm continues, God has crowned humanity with *"glory and honor,"* putting *"everything in subjection"* under our feet. Everything means everything. We may not yet see the full scope of all the things that will be placed under humanity's rule and dominion. However, that is our destiny and ultimate inheritance. Even the angelic hosts are included. Humanity is destined to be the supreme ruler of God's creation.

Jesus lived into the temporary humiliation of humanity in that he, too, was subjected to angelic subjugation, even unto death. He was made low in order that he might be crowned. Our "great salvation" was made manifest in his humiliation and exaltation. It was with us and for us. Jesus entered into communion with us, in humility unto death, in order that we might enter into communion with him, in glory unto life.

This communion is reflected in the Eucharist, also termed Holy Communion. The preacher describes how Jesus *"tasted death"* (2:9) and *"partook of flesh and blood"* (2:14). The same language is used by the Apostle Paul in reference to the sacrament of Holy Communion: *"Because there is one bread, we who are many are one body, for we all partake of the one bread"* (1 Corinthians 10:17). As Jesus taught:

> *Truly, truly, I say to you, unless you eat the flesh of the Son of Man and drink his blood, you have no life in you. Whoever feeds on my flesh and drinks my blood has eternal life, and I will raise him up on the last day. For my flesh is true food, and my blood is true drink. Whoever feeds on my flesh and drinks my blood abides in me, and I in him.*

JOHN 6:53-56

Jesus shared in the flesh and blood of human life and death that we might share in the glory and power of divine life. In another place the Apostle Peter describes how we will become *"partakers of the divine nature" (2 Peter 1:4).* He communes with us that we might commune with him.

Reflection:

Think about your place in the universe and your place in God's plan. How can you shape your daily life to reflect both Jesus' humbling himself for your salvation and God's great plan for humanity?

THE LORD BE WITH YOU

There is an old joke about a priest who starts shouting into the microphone in church saying, "Is this thing on?" He makes lots of noise and finally says, "Something is wrong with this mic!" And the congregation replies: "And also with you."

I have noticed that the salutation and response of the worship service, "The Lord be with you," followed by, "And also with you" is often used to gain the attention of boisterous crowds. I have heard it used at potlucks and coffee hours to quiet the masses. Perhaps we should remember its significance.

"The Lord be with you" (from the Latin, *Dominus vobiscum*) is an ancient salutation that has been used in Christian liturgy since at least the time of the Church fathers. The traditional response is "And with thy spirit" (from the Latin, *Et cum spiritu tuo*), which in many modern liturgies has been rendered, "And also with you." This call and response is used in the Bible as a greeting.

In the context of a worship service, what may sound like a polite greeting is a profound acknowledgement of the presence of Jesus Christ in the gathered people of God—and in the one who presides. The phrase "And with thy spirit" more aptly conveys that the minister who presides over the worship service is doing so *in persona Christi* (Latin, *in the person of Christ*). The Spirit of the Lord is present in the gathered worshiping community and especially in the one who presides. The early Church father John Chrysostom understood this significance:

> If the Holy Spirit were not in our Bishop [referring to Bishop Flavian of Antioch] when he gave the peace to all shortly before ascending to his holy sanctuary, you would not have replied to him all together, "And with your spirit." This is why you reply with this expression … reminding yourselves by this reply that he who is here does nothing of his own power, nor are the offered gifts the work of human nature, but is it the grace of the Spirit present and hovering over all things which prepared that mystic sacrifice.
> (Pentecost Homily)

In the Roman tradition, it is often argued that the salutation is to be reserved for usage only to the ordained clergy—bishops, priests and deacons—as the response "And with thy spirit" acknowledges a special and unique charism or gifting only given in ordination to those called to preside over liturgical rites.

The more Protestant churches see all members as being able to minister "In the person of Christ" because of the priesthood of all believers. Hence, the more modern translation is perhaps truer to a Protestant understanding when it adds the word "also" to the traditional response. "The Lord be with you" … "And *also* with you." The same Spirit of the Lord Jesus which is present in the lay people of God is *also* present in the ordained presider, or celebrant.

The salutatory dialogue is a recognition that Jesus Christ is present in all the ministers of the liturgy, both in the laity and in the ordained clergy. Neither the presider nor the congregation of worshipers can minister in the sanctuary of the Lord in their own power and flesh; it is by the grace of the Spirit of the Lord Jesus Christ present and hovering over all things that we manifest acceptable worship.

Day 5

THE EMPATHY OF JESUS | Read Hebrews 2:10-18

A few months ago, a man came into my office seeking help. With his head hung low and his eyes brimming with tears, he explained how the death of a loved one had left him with a loneliness and sorrow weighing heavily on his heart, suffocating him with grief. He told me, hands shaking, that he wanted to just waste away and die—no one would miss him, he said. The few people he'd reached out to had merely offered advice: read the Bible more and go to church on Sundays. And while the Bible and the body of the Church offer comfort, this man needed something more. He needed empathy, someone to listen to him with an open heart and engage with him in brotherly intimacy.

In Hebrews 2:10-11, the preacher explains the empathy and fellowship we have in Jesus: "*For it was fitting that he, for whom and by whom everything exists, in bringing many sons to glory, should make the founder of their salvation perfect through suffering. For he who sanctifies and those who are sanctified all have one source. That is why he is not ashamed to call us brothers.*" Without hesitation, Jesus claims us as his own. He knows how difficult human life can be. He's been there, seen it all, and he can relate.

God knew that we humans, with our oft-closed hearts and propensity for sin, needed a savior that understood the suffering we experience. Hebrews 2:14-15 explains that, because Jesus shared our humanity "*in flesh and blood,*" he can free us from our fear of death *and from death itself.* Human feelings of loneliness and shame come from fear—fear of inadequacy, of embarrassment, of failure, and, at the root of it all, fear of death. Everyone has felt afraid and ashamed at some point in their lives. But the preacher of Hebrews tells us that Jesus can free us from those shackles.

You see, though fear binds us to death, Jesus is the key that releases us from those chains. His empathy for our fear and his deep understanding of our humanity allow him to take us from the prison of death into loving intimacy with God. Because his empathy is the key to intimacy, God works through Jesus to draw us closer to himself. Only by opening our hearts to Jesus, just as he opened his to us, can we begin to cultivate an intimate relationship with God.

Intimacy with God is the ultimate goal. As Christians, we strive to create and maintain a relationship with God. Ideally, everything we do should glorify him. But temptations are great, and it's easy to succumb to our human emotions. That's why God sent Jesus down to earth—in order that we might have someone who empathizes with us, someone to save us. He sent us a son who, while on earth, acted in time and space as the middleman between perfect divinity and flawed humanity.

But though we can empathize with him, Jesus is also the High Priest, the conqueror of death, and the destroyer of the devil. He atoned for our sins by paying our debt with his earthly life, and through that ultimate sacrifice, proved his place as God's Son.

Jesus is a holy being who claims us as his own. He calls us his *"brothers."* He vibrantly and clearly claims us as his own family to everyone. He joins with us and calls us to join him in family praise of God the Father. How could we not reciprocate his love? How could we instead harden our hearts? How could we reject Jesus' empathetic invitation to true intimacy with the Father?

Once we accept Jesus' radical empathy, we can commune with him and create a deep and lasting relationship. This relationship with Jesus only brings us closer to God because the more effort we make to be intimate with Jesus, the more intimate our relationship with the Father and Spirit becomes.

Overcoming Temptation

In this passage of Hebrews, the preacher identifies Jesus as our savior, priest, and defender. He also shows how Jesus has already claimed us as his own and now considers us his brothers and sisters. The good news is: He has lived through your temptations and can empathize.

But don't forget that the Bible calls for us to model Jesus' behavior in our own lives. Jesus can also help us here, empowering us to live as we ought and to overcome temptation.

In 1 John 2:6, John tells us that *"whoever says he abides in him ought to walk in the same way in which he walked."* According to the preacher to the Hebrews, one important way we can *"walk"* like Jesus is to show the same empathy to others as he shows to us. So, reach out to a friend who might be struggling. Pay attention to the people you meet, and meet them with an open heart. Listen to those around you and try to relate. Remember, Jesus' empathy extends far beyond just a few people—everyone in the family of God is his brother and sister, which means that they are yours, and mine too. When you share vulnerably in life's struggles with others, you're taking the first step towards intimacy on a personal level. But you're also showing the love that Jesus offers us all through his sacrifice.

Reflection:

Jesus is the ultimate empathizer, and through him, we reach intimacy with God. Do you feel closer to God when you contemplate how Jesus empathizes with you? Reflect on a time when you showed empathy toward someone and it deepened the relationship. How did it feel to communicate openly and honestly, sharing in the suffering of another?

Day 6

Beginning in chapter 3, the focus of Hebrews shifts to an argument for the supremacy of Jesus above human prophets, specifically Moses. In the days of the Old Testament, prophets like Moses were highly revered, and rightly so, since they were eye-witnesses to the amazing acts of God and his angels. Since the arrival of Jesus, however, it was necessary for the preacher of Hebrews to clarify to believers the status of Jesus as the Son of God compared to the prophets of old.

The preacher uses the metaphor of a house to explain the places of Jesus and Moses in God's kingdom. If God's kingdom is a house, then Jesus, the son of the master of the house, holds a higher rank than Moses, a servant. Though Moses was faithful to *"testify to the things that were to be spoken later,"* he was a servant nonetheless (Hebrews 3:5).

God's house is a metaphor for the kingdom he is building (*"the builder of all things is God"* Hebrews 3:4). And God's house is not an empty house. Nor is it a house with only servants and one master. He created a house with someone in-between, someone to bring guests to him—a High Priest, Jesus. God built this house with the help of his servants, like Moses. He also built it for the eventual arrival of his Son, in order that believers in him would have a safe, sacred space in which to enter into holy intimacy with their Lord.

The preacher uses the image of a house because, in the Old Testament, God tells Moses to build a tent of meeting so the Israelites can have a place to worship. This tent was a physical space for meeting with God. It eventually became the temple. But with the arrival of Jesus Christ, the preacher explains, the house of God has become immaterial in nature—an expansion of the physical temple.

Now, those drawn in by Jesus make up the house itself. Wherever

Christians gather to worship, they manifest God's house. You see, God's house doesn't reference a physical church building. God's house is spiritual, made of the living stones of the worshippers. The term describes a gathering in sacred communion with God through Jesus. God created a way to communicate with us through Jesus, and whenever we enter into communion with Jesus by opening our hearts and minds to him, we enter the house of the Lord of Lords.

When we meet together in a service of worship, Jesus is the one who speaks the Gospel, inviting us into God's inner chamber, just as the High Priest in the Old Testament brought the needs of the people into the Holy of Holies. Jesus is the key to the inner sanctum, the one opening the curtain to the Most Holy Place. He is both the messenger and the High Priest.

God's house can also be described as the Sabbath rest. The Sabbath rest doesn't just refer to a specific day of rest—the word also encapsulates the sacred time and space set aside to reflect and communicate with God. Whether that Sabbath takes place at a communion rail on Sunday morning, your nightly prayer, or a few hours of Bible study each week, any time set aside expressly for intimacy with God offers you the opportunity to enter his house.

But we cannot access Sabbath rest without holding fast to our convictions. The preacher makes it clear that followers of Christ are part of his house only when we *"hold fast our confidence and our boasting in our hope"* (Hebrews 3:6). So, how do we remain steadfast in our confidence and hope in God?

Paul writes in his letter to the Romans, in verse 1:16, *"For I am not ashamed of the Gospel, for it is the power of God that brings salvation to everyone who believes."* Paul preached the Gospel despite the obstacles the world threw at him. He confessed his faith in Jesus, and through his constant proclamations, forged a powerful relationship with God through intimacy with Jesus. Luke 12:8-9 says something similar: *"I tell you, everyone who acknowledges me before men, the Son of Man will also acknowledge before the Angels of God."* Confession of faith with and among others is a requirement for entry and participation in God's house. The Bible makes it clear: when Jesus invites you into God's house—into the quiet, holy sanctity of spiritual intimacy and salvation—you must accept his invitation by publicly proclaiming your faith in him.

But beware: the world loves to shame those who eagerly profess their beliefs, especially Christians. It's common these days to feel real opposition to a Christian life lived publicly. But accepting the shame destroys intimacy with God, rotting it from the inside out. Instead, if we refuse to accept shame for proclaiming our confidence and hope God, we can enter into holy intimacy with him and be saved from fear and death through Jesus.

Yesterday, you read about creating intimacy with God through empathy with Jesus. But that empathy can only be reached by opening your heart and joyfully confessing your faith in him, by being part of his house. How can you enter the house of God if you are too timid to boldly claim his Son, to shout Jesus' name from the proverbial rooftops? He has already claimed you by paying your debts in full through his death! To participate in the intimacy of God, you must claim him back.

Reflection:

Think about your habits—do you consciously set aside time to enter the holy space of Sabbath rest outside of the Sunday service? Do you feel like you are living up to the standard of confident and steadfast hope in Jesus Christ? Is anything or anyone hindering you from making a bold public confession of Jesus?

Day 7

After the Israelites escaped Egypt, they faced a long journey across treacherous terrain in their quest to reach the Promised Land. Every morning, they shook the sand out of their sandals and steeled themselves for the day's walk, fixing their sights on the horizon. They felt hunger gnaw at their bellies and thirst dry their throats, but the promise of Sabbath rest in God's kingdom sustained them as they walked miles each day. And eventually, they saw it right before them—the Promised Land, not a mirage this time, but the real destination of their trek.

So the Israelites sent their scouts to check out the walled cities of the Promised Land, but when the scouts came back, they told terrifying stories of the giants who inhabited the land. The Israelites became fearful. They had no great army—they were weak from traveling and extremely low on supplies. How could they fight giants? Some started to suggest they turn back, saying, *"Would it not be better for us to go back to Egypt?"* (Numbers 14:3). And because they were hungry, thirsty, exhausted, and afraid, more and more of the group began to wonder if they should turn around after all.

In their fear, they forgot that God was on their side. They forgot that God had promised them the sacred land! They stopped trusting in God and disobeyed him. They chose not to go forward because of fear, and God made sure they wandered in the desert for forty years until all the doubters died off. By then, a new generation of faithful and obedient people was ready to enter the Promised Land. The Israelites who left Egypt were supposed to go from the chaos of the desert to Sabbath rest in the Holy Land, but their entrance into God's land was delayed by doubt and disobedience.

The book of Numbers tells this story and the preacher of Hebrews references the disobedient and doubting Israelites as a warning about what can happen when you harden your heart to God. He implores the Hebrews to remember the story, to avoid becoming like the fearful generation who wandered the desert. The warning then and now is against an "*evil, unbelieving heart.*" Those with hard hearts cannot enter God's rest, just like the generation of Israelites who disobeyed could not enter the Holy Land.

God is described throughout the book of Hebrews as "the Living God." He is not a religious idol or a concept or a philosophy. God is alive, speaking to us, calling to us, and inviting us into a personal relationship with him, through the Son, in the power of the Holy Spirit. The preacher to the Hebrews reminds his listeners that we have a daily choice to stay with the Living God and press on towards Sabbath rest or to drift away. We stay with the Living God by trusting and obeying him.

How do we know God is worthy of our trust? Because he has demonstrated his love and trust to us by sending his Son to save us. He has given us a way to find complete peace in him. The Sabbath rest described in the story of the Israelites refers to their journey to the physical Holy Land, but when God gave us Jesus, he gave us a way to enter the mystical Promised Land without regard to our personal proximity to the Holy Land. Just as Moses led the Israelites from the bondage of Egypt to the Sabbath rest of the Promised Land, Jesus is leading us out of an even greater bondage to Satan and sin to an even greater Sabbath rest in the Promised Land of a New Jerusalem. This leading of Jesus is an act of God's great love.

We have a choice to reciprocate his love by trusting that his plan is greater than our fear and by obeying the commands he has set before us. The preacher to the Hebrews makes it clear that our choice is a *daily* one. Every day, we must make the conscious decision to stay with the Living God, and we must encourage our brothers and sisters in Christ to do the same. It is only through daily renewal of our commitment to God that we keep our hearts open to him.

Consider the word "encourage." It comes from the 15th century French word *encoragier* ("en" meaning *to strengthen* and "corage" meaning *heart.)* Literally it means, "to strengthen the heart." The preacher of Hebrews calls for followers of Christ to encourage one another so that they might not fall away from the Living God. Paradoxically, a hardened heart is a weak heart. We are called to "strengthen the hearts" of our brothers and sisters so that our hearts will remain soft to the will of God and determined to do his will. It is a daily choice, to soften, to strengthen, but it is one that comes with a great reward.

God's people of old failed where we can succeed. They hardened their hearts to the promise, even though God was leading and purposing to bless them. We are still *"hearing his voice"* today and we need to learn a lesson from the Israelites. Rather than shrinking back with hearts hardened by fear, we need to encourage one another to keep our hearts open and receptive to the Lord. In this case, soft hearts are strong hearts, holding firm our confidence in God. In this way, the preacher assures, we come to *"share in Christ,"* or as the King James Version puts it, we become *"partakers of Christ."*

Reflection:

In this day and age, we face different temptations and fears than the Israelites did. But we still experience circumstances that challenge the strength of our hearts. What makes our hearts hardened by fear toward the Lord? What is preventing you from softening your heart and encouraging others to do the same?

Week 2

ENTERING FEARLESSLY INTO SABBATH REST

So then, there remains a Sabbath rest for the people of God, for whoever has entered God's rest has also rested from his works as God did from his. Let us therefore strive to enter that rest, so that no one may fall by the same sort of disobedience.

HEBREWS 4:9-11

Day 8

THE PROMISE OF REST | Read Hebrews 4:1-11

In chapter 4, the preacher makes the case from the Scriptures that the term "*today*" in Psalm 95 means that there is still a Sabbath rest ahead for us to enter.

What is the ultimate Sabbath rest for the people of God? It is resting from our labor in Christ.

As we come into the presence of the Living God in a worship service, the Holy Spirit speaks to us through the liturgy of the word. The aim is, through the softening of our hearts, to lead us willingly into the throne room of the Lord of the Sabbath—the Living God who rests from his creative work and beckons us to join him. Are we responsive to the call, are the occupations and distractions of this world preventing us from truly engaging with the Holy?

This is a powerfully relevant message for Christians in our day. Many remain immature because, though they've learned the basics and gone through the rights of baptism and confirmation, they stay shallow. They do not *press on* into the holiness of life. They ignore the intimacy with God through Jesus Christ to which they're called. The writer of Hebrews uses the context and backdrop of worship to issue this exhortation to move toward Sabbath rest and not fall back in disobedience. As we move toward Christian maturity and Sabbath rest, the fundamental goal is worship. The Presbyterians have a catechism where they say, "What is the chief end of man? Man's chief end is to glorify God, and to enjoy him forever." (Westminster Shorter Catechism, 1647)

In his *Reflections on the Psalms*, CS Lewis develops the idea that to worship and glorify God *is* to enjoy him. If you enjoy God, you will glorify him because we praise what we enjoy. Someone who's just read a great novel might say, "I love this book. You've got to read it." Or someone who's just been hiking might urge, "Look at this photo! Isn't the view breathtaking?" My dad loves to fish. He's so enthusiastic that he can get anyone fired up about fishing just because he enjoys it so much. He "worships" it. It's the same thing with lovers. Lovers never stop confessing their love and admiration for the beloved who delights them. When we give compliments to the people we love to be with, we are glorifying them. And it brings them joy that we delight in them.

> 'Mid toil and tribulation,
> And tumult of her war,
> She waits the consummation
> Of peace for evermore;
> Till, with the vision glorious,
> Her longing eyes are blest,
> And the great Church victorious
> Shall be the Church at rest.
> Yet she on earth hath union
> With God the Three in One,
> And mystic sweet communion
> With those whose rest is won
> O happy ones and holy!
> Lord, give us grace that we,
> Like them, the meek and lowly,
> On high may dwell with Thee.[1]

To glorify God is to delight in him and enjoy him. *This is the fundamental end of what it means to be a Christian and to walk with God.* Our hearts long to not only hear his voice, but to walk with him in the cool of the day, as Adam did. Remember Adam in the garden? He could intimately commune in fellowship with the Lord in the cool of the morning—this is what the end of restoration is like. Sabbath rest is the day provided to enjoy God fully. It is all about enjoyment of fellowship with God, the day that we simply rest and delight in being in his presence and in the presence of the people of God. The ultimate Sabbath rest is to *"enjoy him forever."*

---

[1] The Church's One Foundation, Samuel John Stone (1839-1900)

Eternal enjoyment in God is what we're all working toward. It's what we're trying to enter that ultimate Sabbath rest where we can be together with God, at peace and content in his presence forever. We journey towards this perpetual peace in eternity, but it is also something we can and should join in every time we enter into Christian worship. We partake in Sabbath rest when we come together; when, without impatience or distraction, we enter a moment where we can hear God speaking to us. Here, our hearts are receptive and attentive to his voice, and we respond with belief, praise, petition, and confession. When this takes place, we enter a deeper phase, communion, in which we partake in a banquet together and enjoy fellowship with the Lord in his presence. This is what the writer of Hebrews is encouraging the Church to do.

The Eucharist, the celebration of the Holy Communion, includes the simple elements of bread and wine because the Lord knew that this basic meal would bind us together in fellowship. God invites us to enjoy him by sitting at his table with our brothers and sisters in Christ, and together share in God's presence.

Reflection:

The Lord seeks to restore in us enthusiasm and pleasure in his presence. What distractions in your life are preventing you from enjoying the Lord? What can you do to find true delight in God and your worship of him?

Day 9

Up to this point, the exhortation of Hebrews has been primarily focused on the Liturgy of the Word. Here is the heart-piercing final encouragement to pay attention to Scriptures!

The heart of the matter is a matter of the heart. Let's be honest—our hearts can harden toward an intimate relationship with God. Over our lifetimes, tragedies, losses, willful rebellion, broken relationships, worry, and fear may all disconnect us from a warm and intimate relationship with the Lord.

Thankfully, God has just the tool to penetrate a hard heart—his word. The word of God is described in today's passage as a living and active two-edged sword. This sword can penetrate through the tough shell of cynicism blocking our hearts and pierce to the core of our beings to convict us of sin.

In the latter half of the 14th century, a young adult approached a wise monk and asked how to truly know and be known by God. In response, the monk wrote a short text entitled *The Cloud of Unknowing.* Now considered one of the classics of Christian mysticism, the book posits that God dwells in an unknowable cloud which can only be penetrated by a heart of love. The monk wrote that the Lord can be loved, but he cannot be thought. By love he can be grasped and held, but by thought, he can neither be grasped nor held. In other words, it is impossible to know God without loving him.

> *And therefore, though it may be good at times to think specifically of the kindness and excellence of God, and though this may be a light and a part of contemplation, all the same, in the work of contemplation itself, it must be cast down and covered with a cloud of forgetting. And you must step above it stoutly but deftly, with a*

devout and delightful stirring of love, and struggle to pierce that
darkness above you; and beat on that thick cloud of unknowing with
a sharp dart of longing love, and do not give up, whatever happens.

THE CLOUD OF UNKNOWING

In other words, a relationship with God will not occur merely as an intellectual exercise or scholarly pursuit. God is wholly relational. We know God when we communicate with our hearts full of love.

As a priest, I know that effective preaching only occurs when the two-edged sword of the word hits its intended target—the heart. I can educate and enlighten, I can entertain and inform, I can encourage and admonish, but if the heart is not enlivened, I will have accomplished little in communicating God's word.

God's word is alive.

The Bible is no dead letter. Today, God speaks through the words of the Holy Scriptures as loudly and clearly as when they were first authored. We worship the Living God. He addresses us through his word and speaks directly to our hearts. The two-edged sword cuts right into the heart of our being, soul, and spirit. Through it, God reveals our thoughts and sheds light on the desires of our hearts.

One of our standing prayers at the beginning of worship every Sunday is the Collect for Purity. It is appropriate to pray this prayer at the beginning of the Ministry of the Word because it recognizes that we cannot enter the act of worship without engaging the Living God.

We prepare for worship because God is about to speak to us! He knows exactly what areas of our minds, hearts, and souls need to be addressed and called to account. There are no secret thoughts or hidden attitudes when we come into the presence of a holy, holy, holy God.

*Almighty God, to you all hearts are open, all desires known, and
from you no secrets are hid. Cleanse the thoughts of our hearts by the
inspiration of your Holy Spirit, that we may perfectly love you and
worthily magnify your holy name; through Christ our Lord. Amen.*

COLLECT FOR PURITY, THE BOOK OF COMMON PRAYER, P. 355

The desire is that, through the living and active word of God, which is
inspired (literally *"God-breathed"*), God would purify the thoughts of our
hearts. That is an interesting idea, that our hearts would have *"thoughts"*
that need to be perfected. Usually, we associate thoughts with our minds.
But thoughts that require purification find their origin in the heart.

> *For the word of God is living and active, sharper than any two-edged
> sword, piercing to the division of soul and of spirit, of joints and of
> marrow, and discerning the thoughts and intentions of the heart.*

HEBREWS 4:12

To know God is to love God. We think about him spiritually through our
hearts. If the aim is pure worship and intimacy, then we must practice
absolute attentiveness to God in our hearts. God's desire is that we would
truly know him as he truly knows us. Vulnerability before the Lord means
our souls are ever before him. The Psalmist reflects on the all-perceiving
God:

> *You have searched me, Lord,
> and you know me.
> You know when I sit and when I rise;
> you perceive my thoughts from afar.
> You discern my going out and my lying down;
> you are familiar with all my ways.*

PSALM 139:1-3 (NIV)

Remember how Adam and Eve hid from God in their guilt and shame?
Yet the Lord still saw them, knew them, perceived what was in their
hearts. He knows you, sees you, and perceives the thoughts and intentions

of your heart. Allow the living and active word of God to penetrate to your heart's deep and secret inner chambers.

Reflection:

Have you ever been in a worship service and felt as if the Scriptures or the sermon was speaking uniquely to you, directly to your heart? Has a turn of phrase from the Bible or a word preached been used by God to convict you of a specific area needing prayerful attention or urgent repentance? When was the last time you had such an experience? What did you do to respond?

Day 10

The aim of the Liturgy of the Word is to move us into the Liturgy of the Sacrament. As our hearts are convicted and respond to the word (Scripture) spoken to us by the Word (Jesus), the call is to draw in to the presence of the Living God. We do this through the mediation of the Great High Priest, Jesus. Once we hear and understand the Word, we can move toward the sacred rituals of worship.

Beginning with Hebrews 4:14, the focus of the book turns to the second act in the drama of divine worship. The logic is simple: Because Jesus has come to us and shared with us, let us now go with him into the heavenly realms. He came and shared with us in our human weakness that we might go and share with him in the divine throne room of grace.

Many of our New Testament writings were intended to be used in the context of worship. To fully understand their meaning, we must see them through this lens. Much of our perspective on the Scriptures has been shaped by the academic approach of seminaries and universities. Even when a church undertakes in-depth studies of Biblical books, it often does so in a classroom. It is useful to study the word of God with an academic eye, lifting the Scripture out of its original context for a close reading of important parts, but it is an entirely different thing to study the word through practice.

As discussed in the introduction, the writer of Hebrews describes his letter as an exhortation—a sermon. It is intended to speak into the context of a worshiping community. When it is studied without consideration of a community in worship, it remains instructive, but it does not reach its fullest potential—to inspire zealous and faithful worship. Consider a bicycle. You could study a bike and all its parts in a bike shop. You could learn the mechanics of it—how the chain, the spokes, the wheels, and the handlebars are each designed and fit together. However, the only way to fully understand a bike is to use it—to experience it. Take it out on the road for a spin.

The same is true for the sermon to the Hebrews. When we hear a beautiful verse like Hebrews 4:16, *"Let us therefore approach the throne of grace with boldness, so that we may receive mercy and find grace to help in time of need,"* we could contemplate the meaning of the word "grace." Grace is unmerited favor. Everybody needs grace. Isn't it wonderful that God forgives us and that we can come to him anytime we have need? Of course! However, to experience the real power of the verse, we need to hear it for what it is: an invitation to approach the sanctuary of the Lord in the midst of a service of worship. It is the preacher's call to the worshiper to respond to the word of the Lord with active belief: *"...approach the throne of God with boldness."* The corporate hearers are invited to physically get out of their pews and approach the holy table of the Lord's presence to receive his grace and love. What a marvelous invitation! It is a call to a tangible *experience of God* as we partake in the real spiritual and sacramental presence of the Lord.

How many approach the altar rail of the sanctuary without seriously contemplating that they are approaching the throne of a king? How many fail to consider, as they kneel to receive the bread and the wine, that they are approaching the presence of the Holy One, the King of Kings and the Lord of Lords? Without serious awareness of what we are doing and who we are approaching, we will never find the help and mercy that the Holy One alone can give us.

The word of God is written to lead us into a deeper intimacy with the Living God; we must experience it within its intended context. Allow your study of Hebrews to translate directly to the practicalities of your worship of God in and through Jesus Christ. Take what you read and discuss it in the presence of your worshiping community and then live it out in your worship service. Through your study of his word, God is calling you into a deeper relationship with himself. Soften your heart and open your ears to hear and to respond.

Reflection:

What have you taken from your study of Hebrews so far? Think about how you can implement these teachings— how can you deepen your awareness of the Lord during worship?

_____

_____

_____

_____

Day 11

COMPASSION OF JESUS | Read Hebrews 5:1-10

The priest or pastor functions as a mediator between God and people, or as the writer puts it, *"on behalf of men in relation to God"* (Hebrews 5:1). As a mediator, a pastor must have empathy for other people and the struggles of humanity, so pastors must have experience with the challenges of life. It is the very human weakness of these servants of God that make them uniquely qualified to minister to other humans. Because they can relate to the struggles of the flesh and the need for grace, priests and pastors can empathize—"been there, done that." However, the humanity of pastors means they need mediation for their own sins as well as for the sins of those they serve.

While pastors and priests must have empathy and are often drawn to ministry because of the challenges they've faced, their worthiness to serve does not lie in their own strengths or positive qualities. Rather, their qualification rests in God's call and election. Priests and pastors are appointed by God, not self-appointed. In the Old Testament, high priests were chosen by God, which is why the preacher mentions Aaron. Perhaps you've heard stories of modern pastors who have experienced the voice of God calling them into service.

Like the earthly priests of now and ancient high priests of the Old Testament, Jesus also was called into service by God. However, Jesus' call was clearer and more powerful because of his status as the Son of God. When John the Baptist baptized Jesus, everyone present heard the voice of God. Matthew described it this way: *"And when Jesus was baptized, immediately he went up from the water, and behold, the heavens were opened to him, and he saw the spirit of God descending like a dove and coming to rest on him, and behold, a voice from heaven said, 'This is my beloved Son, with whom I am well pleased'"* (Matthew 3:16-17). By identifying Jesus as his Son in such a public and verbal way, God gave Jesus the divine authority he needed to justify his place as the highest priest.

The preacher to the Hebrews emphasized Jesus' empathy earlier in the book not just to prove Jesus' accessibility and open heart for those in need, but also as a way to validate Jesus' status as high priest. Like human priests, Jesus' humanity is essential because he can relate to us and *"deal gently with the ignorant and wayward, since he himself is beset with weakness"* (Hebrews 5:2). Jesus' passion on the Cross was in sympathy with our weakness. As he called out in pain to God, he demonstrated his unique qualification of perfection in the midst of suffering, through his obedience to God's will. Though he was human, Jesus remained true by trusting and obeying God through the most difficult of ordeal—his sacrificial death on our behalf. Because of his *"loud cries and tears,"* Jesus is a perfect priest. He humbled himself, allowing his time on earth to give him the empathetic qualifications he needed to understand humans and deal mercifully with them as his high priest, and God's call gave him the divine authorization to rule as his Son, the King.

The name Christ comes from two words, the Greek root *khriein* meaning "anoint" and the Hebrew title *"masiah"* meaning "Anointed One." Those words were combined in Greek as *Khristos* and subsequently became the Latin *Christus,* Old English *Crist,* and finally, the modern *Christ.* It's important to remember that Jesus' name comes from "anointed" because, at the time, prophets, priests, and kings were anointed with oil to symbolize their divine authority through God. Jesus' status as both high priest and king means he was one of the only "priest-kings" in the history of God's rule. The only other priest-king was Melchizedek, which is why God says, *"You are a priest forever after the order of Melchizedek"* (Psalm 110:4). Jesus was anointed with the Holy Spirit by God as his Son, the Lord of Lord and King of Kings.

Though Jesus' status is clear to us in this modern day, the pastor to the Hebrews was preaching in a time when Jesus' place was less of a given. He was explaining Jesus' place as the Son of God and *why* that is important to worship. He was clarifying *how* God wants us to worship him through his Son. He was doing all this in order that the Hebrews might find true salvation and peace and not fall away from the faith. The preacher wants us to remember that Jesus is our high priest and, like our human priests, will understand and empathize with us when we bring him our questions, fears, and worries. But also, he wants us to remember that Jesus is more than a priest! He is an emissary of God, a glorious priest-king who will bring us to salvation in God's kingdom. He will save those who trust and obey him.

Jesus' humanity is essential to his understanding of our struggles and his role as supreme priest. His cries to God and his demonstration of suffering reflect his perfection as our perfect high priest and Savior. By softening our hearts to the divine priest, we accept his place as Lord of our hearts. Once we accept Jesus and find solace in his empathy and love, we are blessed, for Psalm 2:12 says, *"Blessed are all who take refuge in him."*

Reflection:

Just as Jesus has empathy for us, so ought those who serve him in the Church as priests and pastors. Think back to your interactions with members of the clergy—when was the last time you experienced a moment of empathy with a pastor? Do you ever seek advice from them outside of the sermon? If not, what is keeping you from doing so?

Day 12

SOLID FOOD | Read Hebrews 5:11-14

The Christian life involves a process of maturity and growth. Just as a child begins life with immature food for an immature body, so new Christians begin with simple spiritual "food." And just like children, as believers mature, they must consume more mature food to grow strong and healthy. Such food is found in deeper teaching.

The Church initially created two sets of instruction to help incorporate believers into the faith. The first set of instructions were for the pre-baptized and included teaching about repentance and the significance of Baptism. This process of teaching and learning culminated with Lent—a season of preparation. During the Lenten season leading up to Easter, new believers engaged in a series of preparatory rites including acts of confession and repentance as well as exorcism, all leading up to their baptism. At the end of Lent, during the Easter vigil service, everyone who had been preparing to join the Church would be baptized. Easter Day celebrated the victory and the welcoming of the newly baptized!

The second set of teachings were for the newly baptized. They provided a deeper lever of instruction on how to grow in intimacy with God through regular worship in the Holy Spirit. They eventually included deeper discussion on the significance of the sacraments of Baptism and the Lord's Supper.

A more developed example of this two-phased instruction is preserved for us in the writings of St. Cyril of Jerusalem. The first half of his teachings are called "Procatechesis"—a series of 18 teaching lectures addressed to the candidates during their preparation for baptism. After their baptisms, five additional lectures were delivered to these new converts. These were called the "Mystagogical Catechesis" and explained the Sacramental Mysteries to the newly-baptized.

How does the book of Hebrews fit into this instruction to believers? Hebrews represents an early example of liturgical instruction for those who have already been baptized but need further elucidation of the meaning of the sacraments and the role of liturgy in their personal and corporate life. The pastor to the Hebrews uses the early Church's instruction about baptism and worship as the backdrop of the letter. He urges followers of Jesus to move on from the "procatechesis" to the "mystagogical catechesis." In other words, he calls for them to move beyond the basic teachings given to them as catechumenates in preparation for baptism to deeper teachings about the significance of worship and sacraments.

The Shape of the Liturgy

In the early Church, there were two main parts of a worship service: The Liturgy of the Catechumenate and The Liturgy of the Faithful. While we do not use these names in our Western tradition, we continue to preserve these two main forms of liturgical worship of God. In the Book of Common Prayer, these two main parts of the worship service fall under the headings: The Word of God and The Holy Communion.

Liturgy of the Catechumenate

The first portion of the ancient worship service, The Liturgy of the Catechumenate, would include singing, Scripture readings, exhortations, and preaching and prayers. At the conclusion, those who were not yet baptized would receive prayers on their behalf that the Lord would be merciful to them, teach them his truth, and reveal his Gospel to them in order that they might be saved in unity with the Church. In the ancient practice, people who were being catechized (preparing to be baptized and join the Church) would be allowed to participate in The Liturgy of the Catechumenate (now called the Ministry of the Word of God). They could hear the Scriptures read and they could receive the instruction from the sermon. However, they would be barred from partaking of The Liturgy of the Faithful (The Ministry of the Sacrament or The Holy

Communion) until they were baptized. The unbaptized would be invited to leave the worshiping assembly during the time of Holy Communion.

From the earliest days of the Church, the unbaptized and uninitiated were not permitted to take communion. From Justin Martyr's *First Apology*, chapter 66 (155 A.D.), we read perhaps the first description of the early Church's "fencing the table" and reserving communion for only baptized believers: "And this food is called among us the Eucharist of which no one is allowed to partake but the man who believes that the things which we teach are true, and who has been washed with the washing that is for the remission of sins, and unto regeneration, and who is so living as Christ has enjoined."

Justin Martyr identifies three prerequisites for the partaker of the Eucharist:

1. One who *believes* that the things which we teach are true.
2. One who has been *washed* with the washing that is for the remission of sins, and unto regeneration.
3. One who is *living* as Christ has enjoined.

Notice that water baptism was not the only prerequisite to partake in Holy Communion. The sincerity of true believing and authenticity of Christian living also were required for access to the table.

Thus, until converts mastered the basic tenants and practices of the faith, they would not be permitted to receive Holy Communion. Even after baptism, converts to the faith needed to go through a teaching and discernment process before being admitted into the full membership of the Church. New converts to the faith needed to be instructed and tested.

Using the food metaphor, the pastor to the Hebrews identifies this first instruction as "milk," the food required for early growth, but eventually outgrown. The "solid food" is what the initiated should consume. Once you have matured and joined the corporate body of the Church, you should no longer simply practice the Liturgy of the Catechumenate. That opening liturgy is meant to move you toward something deeper—the Liturgy of the Faithful, the Ministry of Holy Communion.

One of the best ways to become mature in faith is to teach others. The pastor encourages mature believers to move from the position of student to the role of teacher, leading the uninitiated into the fold. We should all strive to become teachers rather than perpetual students, leading others deeper into intimacy with Christ while sustaining ourselves on the solid food of the Eucharist and other practices of the Faithful.

Reflection:

What can you do to teach others what it means to lead a Christian life? Do you ever find yourself falling back on the "milk" of overly basic teaching? How can you move toward more "solid food?"

Day 13

In the early Church, the catechized would not be admitted to communion to "taste the heavenly gift" until after baptism. Before their baptism, the catechized would learn about the 6 basic principles called the elementary doctrines of Christ. They are:

1. Repentance from Dead Works
2. Faith Toward God
3. Instruction on Baptisms
4. The Laying on of Hands
5. Resurrection of the Dead
6. Eternal Judgement

These 6 foundational teachings are the core of basic catechism class for new converts to the faith who are preparing for baptism. Once they have learned all 6 principles and completed the other requisites for initiation, they are baptized, reborn in Christ. Once a person has gone through the conversion process and the initiation rites of the faith, it is impossible to go back through them again. They have, in a sense, died with Christ on the Cross and risen with him through the waters of baptism.

> *And this we will do if God permits. For it is impossible to restore again to repentance those who have once been enlightened, who have tasted the heavenly gift, shared in the Holy Spirit, and have tasted in the goodness of the Word of God and the powers of the age to come if they then fall away, since they are crucifying once again the son of God.*

HEBREWS 6:3-6

The pastor to the Hebrews is arguing that, just as we cannot go back to re-learning those 6 principles, we cannot be re-baptized. To re-baptize someone has a most dangerous implication of *"crucifying once again the Son of God to their own harm and holding him up to contempt"* (Hebrews 6:6). There is only moving forward in faith—no going backward!

Think of it like this: as young people, we learn about the rite of marriage and the intimacy we will share with our spouse after the ceremony. People teach us about proper intimacy within the context of marriage and, though we learn about it, we will not experience it until after marriage. Once you have married, you share a bond with your spouse that you don't share with anyone else. It's sacred, and together you have a consummate and all-encompassing intimate relationship. However, if your spouse decides to attempt to live a single life again during your marriage, it weakens the bond between you. By falling away from the marriage, the wayward spouse cheapens the ceremony and denigrates the promise they made to you and to your life together. Sometimes the bond, once broken, cannot be mended.

The same is true of our life in Christ. We learn about the word of God and what it means. We then choose to devote our lives to Jesus. We undergo the rite of baptism to effectively mark our rebirth and renewed life, wash away our sins and, by that action, promise our hearts to God. If we turn away from God after making that sacred promise, we compromise our intimate relationship with him. While it is true that most churches will allow those who have fallen away from Christianity a chance to recommit their lives to God, the writer of Hebrews reminds us that this is not the ideal. Even though a wife will sometimes take back a cheating husband, their relationship will never be the same.

The pastor uses a striking image to warn Christians about falling away from God. There are two fields managed by a farmer: the first soaks up all the nourishing rain and produces nutritious fruit for the farmer. The second field, despite receiving rain, bears only nettles, weeds, and bad fruit. When the farmer sees the second field, he burns it in the hope that the fire will cleanse the field.

This illustration vividly paints the picture: a true Christian will soak up the teaching of God's word and the Church, be receptive, and bear the marks of maturity—good fruit. But the person exposed to the teaching of the faith who then neglects to live the Christian life in worship and obedience will not receive salvation but will face potential destruction.

Paul issues a similar call in Ephesians 4:20-24, warning his readers about falling away from God:

> *"But that is not the way you learned Christ!— assuming that you have heard about him and were taught in him, as the truth is in Jesus, to put off your old self, which belongs to your former manner of life and is corrupt through deceitful desires, and to be renewed in the spirit of your minds, and to put on the new self, created after the likeness of God in true righteousness and holiness."*

You wouldn't come home from running on a hot day and go to the trouble of stripping off your sweaty clothes and showering just to put them back on again after drying off. Putting the dirty, sweaty clothes back on means your shower served little purpose! In the same way, Paul argues that you shouldn't put the clothes of the world back on once being bathed in the salvation of Jesus. You must wear the new clothes, put on the "new self"—the righteous and holy self, created in God—and cast away your old self.

All of this is to say: You must keep the faith, choose God every day, grow in your relationship with God, and nurture your righteous self continually… *"lest you drift away."*

Reflection:

Do you ever feel yourself falling away from God? What do you do in those moments to bring yourself back to the righteous track?

Day 14

FULL ASSURANCE | Read Hebrews 6:9-12

There is no way to really see what is taking place in the internal realm of the heart. Even doctors, trained cardiologists, can only examine the flesh and blood of our heart muscle. No amount of knowledge or practice can give a person the ability to glean the inner workings of someone else's spiritual heart. While God can see the thoughts and intentions of our hearts, the only way other people can perceive them is by the fruit of our lives, the products of our labor in Christ.

We teach children about the fruit of the Spirit, often using a little song to list the values—love, joy, peace, patience, kindness, goodness, faithfulness, gentleness, and self-control. It's good to instill children with the knowledge of these characteristics, but our hope is that learning about the fruit of the Spirit will actually help them exhibit these traits as they grow.

As a priest, I speak at a lot of funerals. It's not always easy to console grieving people, but I do my best to offer comfort, even though I don't always have proof or assurance of the faith of the loved one. The best funerals are the ones honoring the life of someone who has openly confessed their faith in Christ and whose life bears witness to the Holy Spirit.

A while back, I spoke at the funeral of a woman who was beloved by her friends and family. Her daughter asked that for part of the service I turn the microphone over to anyone who wanted to share the impact her mother had made on their life. I agreed, albeit a bit hesitantly. I was concerned that few people would want to speak, and the daughter might be disappointed. But when the time came, person after person rose from the pews and offered story after story of this woman's generosity, kindness, faithfulness, and zeal for Christ. I could see the joy and love she inspired in the face of each person who spoke.

Ideally, our lives should stand as testament to our relationship with Jesus. However, it is possible for a person to "drink the rain" of the basic principles of Christianity and go through the initiation rites of baptism, but still not truly be a convert from the heart. Those who have fallen away, or lack conviction, bear bad fruit such as thorns and thistles even after good rain has been received.

Assurance of salvation is possible when observable Christian growth in character and behavior is witnessed. In the case of the Hebrews, the preacher points to their work and love in serving the saints in Jesus' name as proof. He urges them to continue to show earnestness and perseverance so they might have *"the full assurance of hope until the end"* (Hebrews 6:11). The preacher realizes it's easy to get tired, easy to fall away, and difficult to sustain zeal.

Have you ever woken up in the morning and felt terribly exhausted, just wrung out from the day-to-day tasks of life? What gets you out of bed on those days? Perhaps your spouse has put the coffee pot on and you're anticipating that first sip. Or maybe you get up just because you have to go to work. Sometimes you can get up and go through the day in a haze, not fully present, just going through the motions.

The writer of Hebrews warns us against a lack-luster spirit, not of physical tiredness, but of spiritual sloth. Sloth is one of the seven deadly sins recognized by antiquity. It means "giving up on the pursuit of the good, the beautiful, and the true." In relation to the Christian faith, sloth is a sluggishness of spirit (Hebrews 6:12) that leads to a gradual falling away. The further you fall, the harder it is to stand back up.

When our spirits falter or hearts become weak, we're called to look to the witness of those who persevere. We must remember the zealous people who kept their faith in the midst of prejudice and persecution, those who continued to do good no matter the circumstances. (Hebrews 11 is a "Hall of Fame" of these faithful saints.) Finding inspiration through our enthusiastic and passionate brothers and sisters in Christ can help restore our zeal for the Lord and renew our energy.

When you're running a marathon or any long distance race, towards the middle your legs start to feel sluggish. You begin to wonder if you can keep going. Those who are faithful cheer you on from the sidelines, offering you inspiration to restore your energy. This marathon is a picture of life with God—as we continue to "run" with Christ, we must not give up when things get tough. We must keep our eye on the goal and keep persevering! We are called not only to run our own races, but to faithfully encourages others who are running, cheering on even stagnant and immature Christians. If you are stagnant yourself, open your heart to the encouragement of the faithful and to Jesus' motivating love.

I'm reminded of a poem by Mary Oliver called *When Death Comes*. She wrote, "When it's over, I want to say all my life/ I was a bride married to amazement. / I was the bridegroom, taking the world into my arms." When you live your life in the blessed assurance of your hope in Jesus Christ, you are bound to God and you will daily experience amazement. You will be astonished by his grace and love. You will bear witness to the Holy Spirit by bearing ripe and rich fruit, and you will confess your faith to others so they might persevere with you. When death comes, you will inherit God's promise of eternal salvation so long as you remain faithful to him and your life testifies to your work in Jesus.

Reflection:

Who in your life inspires you with their witness to God's grace? How do you restore your zeal for Christ when you begin to feel sluggish?

Week 3

ENTERING FEARLESSLY INTO
SABBATH REST

So then, there remains a Sabbath rest for the people of God, for
whoever has entered God's rest has also rested from his works as
God did from his. Let us therefore strive to enter that rest, so
that no one may fall by the same sort of disobedience.

HEBREWS 4:9-11

Day 15

When a politician is sworn into office, he or she places a hand on the Bible. The same is true when people testify in court—they promise, with one hand on the Bible, that they will tell the truth. Have you ever wondered why we use the Bible to make formal promises about our words? It is because we are promising, under the *authority* of the Bible, that we will keep our word and remain true to our promise.

As humans, we often make promises we can't or don't keep. It's happened to everyone at some point or another—perhaps it was trivial, such as promising your spouse you'd mow the lawn on a particular day and forgetting, or maybe you made a serious business commitment on which you couldn't follow through. We are sinners, after all. Because we have all reneged on a promise at least once, we sometimes have a hard time trusting other people to keep theirs. One way to give a promise more weight is to swear by or on something. We swear by something greater than ourselves, something with more authority than we have, in order to imbue the promise with authority. Usually, we swear by God.

When God promises to make Abraham a great nation, he says, *"And I will make of you a great nation, and I will bless you and make your name great, so that you will be a blessing"* (Genesis 12:2). Then he swears by himself, *"By myself I have sworn"* (Genesis 22:16). As there is no one greater than God, he swore by himself, binding himself to his promise to Abraham. He offered Abraham a double confirmation: his blessing and his oath. We, too, are the recipients of a double confirmation by the oath offered in Psalm 110:4: *"The LORD has sworn and will not change his mind, 'You are a priest forever after the order of Melchizedek.'"* This verse, referencing Jesus, promises that Jesus is our eternal priest, like Melchizedek.

God's promise to send Jesus Christ is hinted at throughout the Bible. The book of Isaiah speaks of this promised salvation in a very specific way.

Isaiah describes Jesus in a series of metaphors that correspond to events in Jesus' earthly life. He prophecies about *"a man of sorrow"* who is like *"a lamb that is lead to the slaughter"* (Isaiah 53:3,7). God promised to save his people by sending someone to *"make intercession for the transgressors,"* saving us from our sin, and he does so in Jesus (Isaiah 53:12).

God fulfilled his promise to us of eternal life by sending Jesus Christ. This promised salvation is a firm anchor for our souls. Just as a boat is secured by a dropped anchor, so our salvation is secured because it is anchored to the throne of the Living God. God affixed our salvation to himself in the form of his Son, whom he "cast down" to earth to save us from our sin and death.

Doubt, however, is an inextricable part of the human experience. Many people stray from God because they doubt the salvation that he alone offers. After all, it sometimes seems too good to be true, right? God loves us and sent his Son to offer us eternal salvation; all we have to do is give him our hearts and love him back, in faith and obedience. God promised us everlasting love, and he keeps his promises.

Unlike people, we can be sure that God will keep his promise of eternal salvation. The preacher reminds us that God has proven his faithfulness through his interactions with Abraham. God promised Abraham a great nation and his blessing, and Abraham became a great man who fathered an entire people. If God can follow through with a promise of that magnitude, how could he fail to let us into the intimacy of salvation he promises? The preacher highlights God's promise to Abraham as a way to demonstrate God's commitment to his word and give us the confidence and courage to enter deeper communion with him. As long as we remember that God's promises are unchangeable, we can ward off doubt and fear and feel assured in our salvation.

God sent a tangible human form of hope down to Earth, Jesus, so that we could witness God's commitment to us. Jesus, our great high priest and Savior, serves as our eternal hope that we will one day enter into the Holy of Holies with him. This guarantee of God's promised salvation to us is an anchor for our souls. It is firmly secured to nothing less than the throne of the living God. The one who fixed it there is none other than the object of the promise: Jesus. He is our priest *forever* in the order of Melchizedek.

Reflection:

Do you keep your promises to others like God keeps his promises to his people? How can you show others your trust in God and your salvation through Jesus Christ?

Day 16

In the days of Abraham, several kings were fighting amongst themselves. You may remember that when Abraham and Lot separated, Lot moved his tent close to Sodom and Gomorrah. Half of the squabbling kings had joined forces against the other half and, during the ensuing battles, the kings of Sodom and Gomorrah fled their cities, leaving them vulnerable to attack. Their enemies ransacked these king-less cities and took Lot and all his possessions during the raid. When Abraham heard that his nephew had been taken, he rallied his men and they traveled to rescue Lot. After they redeemed all the stolen possessions and found Lot, defeating the enemies in the process, Abraham found himself with quite a pile of spoils (Genesis 14:8-16).

Abraham then went to the house of the King of Salem, who was called Melchizedek. Genesis 14:18-20 describes their interaction succinctly:

> *And Melchizedek king of Salem brought out bread and wine. (He*
> *was priest of God Most High.) And he blessed him and said,*
> *"Blessed be Abram by God Most High,*
> *Possessor of heaven and earth;*
> *and blessed be God Most High,*
> *who has delivered your enemies into your hand!"*
> *And Abram gave him a tenth of everything.*

There is no other mention of Melchizedek in the Old Testament except for the verse the writer of Hebrews quotes from Psalm 110. The pastor to the Hebrews zeroed in on a small but important passage in Genesis in order to draw a comparison between Melchizedek and Jesus. He reminds us of several key facts regarding Melchizedek:

1. He is king of Salem
2. He is priest of the Most High God
3. He blesses Abraham
4. Abraham tithes to him
5. His name means King of Righteousness
6. He is the King of Peace (Salem)
7. He is without genealogy, birth, or death

The preacher of Hebrews reiterates these facts in order to teach us about the supremacy of the New Covenant in Jesus. In many ways, Melchizedek resembles Jesus. Like Jesus, he reigns over peace and righteousness, and he is a priest of God. He also is *"without father or mother or genealogy, having neither beginning of days or end of life, but resembling the Son of God he continues a priest forever"* (Hebrews 7:3). Jesus is God's eternal son, so he has no genealogy either.

Because of the similarities between Jesus and Melchizedek, some scholars speculate that Melchizedek is a *theophany*. A theophany is a physical manifestation of God—in this case, a pre-incarnate manifestation of Jesus Christ. This theory helps to explain the similarities Melchizedek shares with Jesus, particularly the fact that he is an eternal priest. The only other eternal priest is Jesus. That is why the verse *"The Lord has sworn and will not change his mind, 'You are a priest forever after the order of Melchizedek,'"* is so important (Hebrews 7:17 quoting Psalm 110:4).

When Abraham meets Melchizedek, Melchizedek leads them both in worship. They have bread and wine together—symbolic of Christ's communion to come. They exchange a blessing for a tithe, which is a transaction of worship. By leading Abraham in worship, Melchizedek shows himself as a liturgist. He demonstrates his position as a worship leader. Like Melchizedek, Jesus is our worship leader.

There's one element of this worship they shared that the writer of Hebrews does not mention. The Genesis passage includes the detail of the bread and wine that they shared, but the preacher leaves this out. His omission is conspicuous. Likely it is because he was writing to an audience that would include those who had not yet been baptized, so he left out the particulars of the communion ceremony. In this way, his omission was hidden to the uninitiated but obvious to the initiated.

In my time as a priest, I've noticed that when someone is new to the church, they sit in the back. At one of the churches where I served, there was a small alcove to the side. New people would often sit here, just behind the wall, so they couldn't really be seen. I didn't understand this impulse to distance oneself from the action of the pulpit! Perhaps the newcomers felt shy, embarrassed, or worried they might sit where an established member liked to sit if they chose a place closer to the front. But the preacher is supposed to encourage everyone to draw in and get up close to the worship service. We are called to lean into God and our worship of him. We are to triumphantly approach the altar of the Living God.

As eternal high priests, Jesus and Melchizedek serve as perennial liturgists, perpetually encouraging us to move closer to God. By drawing a comparison between the two, the pastor to the Hebrews shows us how God's plan for our salvation was in the works long before Jesus ever walked the earth.

Reflection:

Has there ever been a time when you felt you needed to sit in the back of the sanctuary? Why? How did you overcome that feeling and move towards the altar of God?

Day 17

TITHES AND BLESSINGS | Read Hebrews 7:4-10

Abraham, the great patriarch of Israel, gave a tithe of his possessions to Melchizedek. He did so because he recognized that, as a high priest, Melchizedek held a superior position. Abraham wished to honor Melchizedek. In return, Melchizedek blessed Abraham. The preacher to the Hebrews says that, through Abraham, Levi and all Abraham's other descendants also tithed to Melchizedek and received his blessing. In other words, Abraham passes down his tithe along with Melchizedek's blessing to all his descendants.

The custom of offering blessings verbally and tangibly is familiar to us. We do so every Sunday when we worship and tithe. A tithe is defined as a tenth of one's income given to the Lord. It is an expression of worship, an offering of reverence and devotion. We give the Lord a portion of our wealth just as Abraham gave Melchizedek a tenth of his riches.

People often think of tithes as a way to keep the church lights on and to compensate for the labor involved in procuring staff and maintaining the buildings, tithing is much more than that! While these funds help the church with material needs, they hold higher significance as a spiritual offering. We bless God at the beginning of the service with the opening statement, "Blessed be God: Father, Son, and Holy Spirit. And blessed be his kingdom, now and forever." To complement this verbal blessing of the Lord, we offer a tangible blessing—our tithes. Tithing is a symbol of our devotion to God.

Mark 12:41-44 tells the story of Jesus' observance of people make their offering at the temple:

> And he sat down opposite the treasury and watched the people
> putting money into the offering box. Many rich people put in large
> sums. And a poor widow came and put in two small copper coins,

which make a penny. And he called his disciples to him and said to them, "Truly, I say to you, this poor widow has put in more than all those who are contributing to the offering box. For they all contributed out of their abundance, but she out of her poverty has put in everything she had, all she had to live on."

The poor widow gave everything she had. The Scripture doesn't say why, but we can deduce that she trusted the Lord to provide for her. What a powerful demonstration of faith! As Jesus points out in this passage, tithing is not about the amount of money you offer. It is about making a meaningful offering to God from a place of devoted love.

Some churches collect the tithes and offerings from the back of the church to the front, moving toward the altar. This is symbolic of the congregation's drawing closer to God. When all the offerings are gathered, they are presented to the priest who physically lifts them up toward God. Liturgically, the priest is offering the tithes to the risen Lord Jesus Christ. Traditionally, the priest says, "All things come of thee, O Lord, and of thine own have we given thee."

In response to our tithes and worship, the Lord offers us his blessing. But what is a blessing?

We know that it's good, but it can be difficult to articulate exactly what a blessing entails. The Oxford English Dictionary defines *blessing* as "God's favor and protection" or "a person's sanction and support." So while we can offer blessings to God, our proffered blessings take the form of sanction, a verbal affirmation of our trust in God. God's blessing toward us is his favor and protection. And, because of Jesus Christ, he also blesses us with eternal salvation. Through the rite of Holy Communion, we come close to the God who promises through Christ to protect us, hold us in his favor, and allow us to enter his kingdom. His blessing is reiterated through the proclamation at the end: "And the blessing of God Almighty, Father, Son and Holy Spirit, be among you and remain with you always."

In the days of Abraham, followers of God tithed to the Lord and blessed him. They experienced God's blessing of faithfulness, but because they did not yet have Jesus, they did not have the access of communion. Communion is essential to receiving the entirety of God's blessing. By dying for our sins, our great high priest performed the ultimate worship of God—he gave himself as the offering. He offered his earthly life as his tithe to God to pay for the sins of humanity. In doing so, Jesus opened the path to God's kingdom forever. Through Jesus, God allows us to enter the Holy of Holies. His blessing now extends far beyond favor and protection and encompasses complete salvation in Christ. By partaking in communion, we not only accept God's favor, protection, and blessing of salvation through Jesus Christ, but we also enter into a deeper intimacy with him.

To sum up, when we demonstrate our devotion to God through our tithes, we act out our faith and devotion in a tangible way. We are blessing the Lord, as he blesses us. The Lord blesses us by inviting us into his favor, protection, and salvation through Jesus. Enter the Holy of Holies and experience intimacy with God through the ritual made possible by Jesus' ultimate sacrifice. His sacrifice of himself was complete. Communion is where we experience this blessing in full.

When we live for the Lord, we see God's blessings throughout our lives. We are able to recognize the work of the Holy Spirit as the source of all good, and we praise God for his favor. The Doxology reflects this adoration: "Praise God from whom all blessings flow; Praise Him, all creatures here below; Praise Him above, ye heav'nly host; Praise Father, Son, and Holy Ghost. Amen."

Reflection:

How does understanding your tithe as a means of blessing God change your thoughts about giving? Do you experience communion as a blessing? Where else do you see God's blessings manifesting in your life?

Day 18

JESUS AS HIGH PRIEST | Read Hebrews 7:11-19

In Exodus 28, God gives Aaron very specific instructions for worship. He describes in great detail the clothing Aaron should wear as high priest and the clothing the other priests should wear. The garments prescribed for Aaron are fine and symbolic—each piece of clothing serves a specific purpose. His ephod (a sleeveless overgarment) bears the names of the sons of Israel engraved on it so he can *"bear the names before the Lord on his two shoulders for remembrance"* (Exodus 28:13). The breastpiece is likewise engraved so Aaron can *"bear the judgement of the people of Israel on his heart before the Lord regularly"* (Exodus 28:30). His robe has bells. The plate on his turban reads, *"'Holy to the Lord"* so Aaron can *"bear any guilt from the holy things that the people of Israel consecrate as holy gifts. It shall regularly be on his forehead, that they may be accepted by the Lord"* (Exodus 28:36,38).

As high priest, Aaron was responsible for making the necessary sacrifices and atonements for the sins of his congregation. The garments were intended to aid in these atonements, which only Aaron and the high priests who came after him could make. But despite donning clothes with symbols of guilt, judgement, remembrance, and atonement, Aaronic high priests remained human; therefore, their sacrifices before the Lord were destined to always fall short.

The Aaronic priesthood was centered around rituals and duty. God set forth specific instructions and the human priests and high priest followed his commands as best they could. They also enforced God's rules as law, and that meant that most followers of God had a relationship with him centered around duty and lawfulness. They did not know God as we know him.

Relationships founded on duty and ritual alone are destined to be hollow. Even if practiced with zeal, without an emotional connection to create a strong bond, the zealousness of worship eventually wanes into sluggish rule following and rote ritual. The law was never meant to save us. It was designed to show us our inadequacies, for "*all have sinned and fallen short of the glory of God*" (Romans 3:23). It is impossible for humans to always follow the law, so following a religion mediated only by law serves to show us our unworthiness before God.

God gave us the power to change our inadequacy by sending Jesus Christ to serve as a new high priest, one who could perfectly atone for our sins and bring us to salvation in God. With the crucifixion of Jesus, the inadequacy of the order of the Aaronic priesthood is superseded and replaced by the order of Melchizedek. The two priesthoods are radically different. The Aaronic priesthood was based on law, while the priesthood of Melchizedek is based on the "*power of an indestructible life*" (Hebrews 7:16). The Aaronic priesthood was temporary, while the order of Melchizedek is "*forever*" ("*Jesus is a priest forever, after the order or Melchizedek.*" *v.17*). This new forever priesthood changes everything about the way the relationship between God and man is mediated.

The law made *nothing* perfect because it was weak and inadequate. It never truly gave the believer access to God. It mostly served to reveal sin and show human weakness and need. God did away with the old system and gave Jesus the unique power to mediate between God and man intimately. He fulfilled his promise to grant the children of God intimacy with him.

Unlike the Aaronic priesthood, where only the high priest could enter the Holy of Holies to communicate with God, Jesus lifts away the curtain and brings us into intimacy in the kingdom of God. Jesus has no need for the garments of Aaron, for he bore the guilt and judgement of all people, once and for all, washing it away with his blood. He needs no adornment for remembrance, nor fine cloth to please the eye of the Lord, for he is the Prince of Peace, the King of Righteousness. This eternal priesthood is far superior to the Aaronic priesthood, for something perfect and eternal is always better than something temporal and flawed. Jesus serves humanity now and forever, offering hope and empowerment through himself.

Though *"all have sinned and fall short of the glory of God,"* we are *"justified by his grace as a gift, through the redemption that is in Christ Jesus, whom God put forward as a propitiation by his blood, to be received by faith"* (Romans 3:23-25). In the Melchizedekian and Messianic eternal priesthood, followers are no longer redeemed *"by a law of works,"* but we find salvation *"by the law of faith"* (Romans 3:27).

The power of indestructible life is what Jesus offers us in his eternal priesthood. Take comfort in knowing that your high priest imparts to you his eternal life in salvation. This is why it is called a *"better hope"*! (Hebrews 7:19).

Reflection:

The Aaronic priesthood focused on law, only highlighting humanity's inadequacy. Through our eternal high priest Jesus, we find salvation— does that give you a *"better hope"?* How does the comparison between the flawed, temporal Aaronic priesthood and Jesus' perfect and eternal priesthood change your understanding of modern worship?

Day 19

THE BETTER COVENANT | Read Hebrews 7:20-28

Because the Aaronic priests were human, the priesthood cycled through priests, establishing a new one as soon as the previous one died. Each priest made sacrifices on behalf of themselves and the congregation. These sacrifices were imperfect and their effectiveness short in the eyes of the Lord. Over time, the daily sacrifices for sin added up to tens of thousands of animals! This priesthood was based on law and overseen by imperfect humans. Though it was established by God's laws, God had plans for an even greater priesthood based this time not on law, but on oath—an oath God swore on his own authority.

Which is better—a law or a promise? At first, you may think laws are better because they help keep society running; their definitive nature makes them useful tools for maintaining order. But, laws are used often to hurt people. They serve mostly to judge our inadequacy and faults (think of the laws against speeding or late payment of taxes). Laws are also deeply impersonal—our cultural image for law, Lady Justice, is depicted blindfolded. She cannot see the person she judges, making her decisions purely impartial.

Promises, on the other hand, are deeply personal. Sometimes promises cross over to the legal realm when they rise to the level of contract, by and large, promises exist between two parties with a personal trust relationship. A promise is meant to be binding, like the law. Oaths (a form of promise) are sometimes sworn under the authority of God. If you make an oath by God (as presidents do when sworn in), that promise holds more power than the law. Because the authority of God reigns supreme over the authority of human government, sworn promises are better than laws.

When God sent Jesus to serve humanity as our high priest, he made good on a promise he'd made to send us someone to intercede on our behalf, a Savior. And he did this by oath: *"The Lord has sworn and will not change his mind…"* (Hebrews 7:21a). What did he swear by oath? *"You are a priest forever,"* referring to Jesus (7:21b). This means that when Jesus died on the cross, his role as high priest didn't end. In God's better oath, he planned for Jesus to act as our priest *eternally*. In this New Covenant, Jesus will continually show us the path to God's kingdom and our salvation. As the preacher sums up, *"This makes Jesus the guarantor of a better covenant"* (7:22). We access the fulfillment of God's promise when we create and maintain an intimate relationship with Jesus Christ.

While God always keeps his promises, humans are flawed. Sometimes we fail to fulfill a promise or fail to follow the law. Usually, the laws and promises we break are innocuous, like jaywalking or forgetting to call someone after setting a time to talk.

Because I serve the Church as a priest, people often ask me to pray for them. I enjoy praying for the people I know and praying on behalf of their loved ones. However, I learned early on in my priesthood that I tend to forget if I put it off. After someone would ask me to pray for them, my immediate impulse was to say, "Yes, I will pray for you," and go on with my day, planning to pray later. But I found that, when I put it off, I ended up not praying for them specifically. Once I realized my weakness as an intercessor, I knew I needed to make a change. I began to pray with people immediately after they asked in order to keep my promise and faithfully serve my community. I've found that praying with people in the moment also strengthens my relationship with them. Though I've found strategies to be a better priest, I am still human and can never be a perfect intercessor. But Jesus is the eternal and perfect intercessor—he not only saves us, but continues to intercede for us with an endless flow of prayer.

Whereas the Aaronic priesthood had imperfect priests who imperfectly sacrificed animals for their own sins and the sins of those they served, Jesus is the perfect high priest. He lived without sin, but he experienced the trials of humanity so that he could understand and give mercy to sinners. He healed the sick and performed miracles while here on earth.

Then, he made the ultimate human sacrifice to absolve humanity of our sin—offering himself, the spotless lamb, one time, in an act sufficient for all. His priesthood, work, and sacrifice are all perfect. The preacher to the Hebrews says that, *"Consequently, he is able to save to the uttermost those who draw near to God through him, since he always lives to make intercession for them. For it was indeed fitting that we should have such a high priest, holy, innocent, unstained, separated from sinners, and exalted above the heavens"* (Hebrews 7:25-26). His eternal power as the highest priest is confirmed by God's oath and remains effective forever.

Because of the power of his indestructible life, Jesus is able to make continual intercession for his people before the throne of God. Our mediator offers us an unending conduit of connection to the Father and the Spirit on our behalf. We who are in him are therefore permanently saved by him, united, and drawn into the triune Godhead: Father, Son, and Holy Spirit.

Reflection:

Do you feel Jesus' endless flow of prayer at work in your life? What kind of relationship do you have with our eternal high priest?

Day 20

The Law of Moses prescribed in detail how the earthly tabernacle or "tent of meeting" would be constructed and furnished. When Moses was on Mount Sinai, God showed him exactly what the tabernacle should look like and Moses built it exactly as God specified. This earthly tent was a mobile throne room, a sanctuary to house the Ark of the Covenant, and a place to worship the Lord. God requires a special meeting place, and the preacher to the Hebrews contends that the pattern God showed Moses was like a shadow of the heavenly throne room, an earthly copy. In fact, the preacher says that the way we worship, the actions of the priests, are but a *"copy and shadow of heavenly things"* (Hebrews 8:5).

God requires a specific meeting place to worship him because Sabbath Rest is about time and space. God's perfect peace lies only in his kingdom. While we cannot physically access his kingdom while living, we can spiritually access his heavenly throne room through communion. It makes sense that our worship spaces emulate God's kingdom as closely as possible as the aim of worship is to draw closer to him. If our earthly sanctuaries and the services within are shadows of the heavenly throne room, imagine how awe-inspiring worship in the heavenly realm must be! In the time before Jesus, worshipers were far from God's heavenly throne room—the only way they could be slightly closer to God was through emulation of his design. But Jesus takes us into the real sanctuary, the sacred Sabbath Rest of God's presence through the intimate ritual of communion.

During church services, the priest invites the congregation into worship with the phrase, "Lift up your hearts." It's implicit in the command that the congregation is lifting their hearts towards God, but what exactly does it mean to lift up our hearts to the Lord? The phrase itself has a long and broad history, woven into many denominations of Christianity. According to the *Oxford Dictionary of the Christian Church, 3rd edition*, the phrase "lift up your hearts" comes from the Latin phrase *Sursum Corda*. Translated literally, it means "Hearts up!" The phrase appears in Christian liturgical materials in the third century; its earliest use is attributed to the *Anaphora of the Apostolic Tradition*. The phrase has inspired hymns, prayers, and sermons, and it remains an important part of worship.

God calls Christians to devote ourselves to him and to seek out and maintain an intimate relationship with Jesus. We offer devotion in the form of tithes and communion, but we also offer up ourselves—we *lift up our hearts*. The word "heart" here obviously does not refer to the organ that pumps our blood; it refers rather to our emotional and spiritual being, the soul we carry within ourselves. We perceive our hearts to be the origin of emotion and passion, and so we offer our emotional selves—our desires, needs, and passions—our most vulnerable parts, to God in worship. By baring our souls to the Lord at the beginning of the service, we show him that we are ready to worship him completely and receive his blessings.

We lift our spiritual hearts into the heavenly throne room, though our physical hearts are beating in the facsimile sanctuary on earth. It takes imagination and eyes of faith to recognize this action—we are placing our hearts on the altar of the God Most High in his heavenly kingdom. Performed with the eyes of faith, lifting your heart to God is an act of true worship as it takes place in the heavenly realm.

We lift our hearts to God *through Jesus*, so that he can wash away their sinful thoughts. Through Jesus alone, we can enter the real sanctuary of heaven. He provides the ultimate intercession by placing our cleansed hearts before his Father. Jesus embodies the New Covenant—indeed, he *"has obtained a ministry that is as much more excellent than the old as the covenant he mediates is better, since it is enacted on better promises"* (Hebrews 8:6).

The preacher to the Hebrews argues that we know that the New Covenant is superior because the Old Covenant was insufficient. It's like the old saying, "If it ain't broke, don't fix it." Why would God offer a new form of something if there was nothing lacking in the old? If the Old

Covenant would suffice, there would have been no need for a new and better promise; so it follows that the New Covenant is inherently better because it replaced an inadequate one.

God's New Covenant is different from the old. It provides eternal salvation where there was formally only temporary and insufficient animal sacrifice for sin. It offers an unbreakable connection with God where there was formerly only disconnected ritual. This New Covenant is ratified in the heart of God's kingdom, before his heavenly throne, and the absolute forgiveness God grants. So there, we lift our hearts up to him.

Reflection:

Do you have the eyes of faith required to see your heart lifted into the heavenly throne room of God? How can you strengthen your spiritual imagination to deepen your connection and intimate relationship with the Lord Almighty?

Day 21

There's an ongoing argument in the worlds philosophy and psychology regarding human nature: are humans intrinsically good or bad? While it's nice to believe that humans are good deep-down, many more philosophers have argued that, though people have a great capacity to be good, we are destined to revert to badness. Biblical philosophy supports this idea with the concept of original sin: because Adam and Eve ate of the fruit of knowledge in the garden of Eden, they were destined to sin as were their descendants. Even the most devout Christians continue to sin, because sinning is an intrinsic part of being human; no matter how much someone desires to be good, they will still do bad things. Remember Romans 3:23, *"for all have sinned and fallen short of the glory of God."*

The prophet Jeremiah held a similar opinion. After watching the suffering of the Israelites, Jeremiah prophesied that people are intrinsically bad, heart-bound to our earthly and evil ways: *"The heart is deceitful above all things, and desperately sick; who can understand it?"* (Jeremiah 17:9). This is the final nail in the Old Covenant's coffin, for if humans will always sin, they will also always require sacrifices to absolve themselves in the eyes of the Lord. The sacrifices made by the high priests were inadequate, and the people cried out for a salvation they could not attain as their hearts were wicked and sacrifices deficient. Who could resolve the problem? The Lord recognized the shortcomings of the Old Covenant and resolved to create an avenue of salvation for his children.

The Lord revealed his plans for a New Covenant to Jeremiah (whom the preacher to the Hebrews quotes in 8:8-12):

> *"Behold, the days are coming, declares the Lord, when I will establish a New Covenant with the house of Israel and the house of Judah, not like the covenant I made with their fathers on the day when I took them by the hand to bring them out of the land of*

*Egypt. For they did not continue in my covenant, and so I showed
no concern for them, declares the Lord. For this is the covenant
I will make with the house of Israel after those days, declares
the Lord: I will put my laws into their minds, and write them on
their hearts, and I will be their God, and they shall be my people.
And they shall not teach, each one his neighbor and each one his
brother, saying, 'Know the Lord,' for they all shall know me, from
the least of them to the greatest. For I will be merciful to their
inequities, and I will remember their sins no more."*

The preacher brings up Jeremiah's prophecy to argue that the New
Covenant was fully anticipated by the Old Covenant. Many other
prophets predicted God's merciful salvation through Jesus, but Jeremiah's
prophecy reveals the why: the Old Covenant was inadequate in that
it failed to achieve its desired result of continual faithfulness in the
knowledge of the Lord. The Old Covenant could not clear the house of
Israel of sin, nor did it truly abide within them. The heart of the problem
with the Old Covenant is a matter of the heart. Because people's hearts
are bad, they required a new and living way of forgiveness.

God offered the New Covenant as a solution to the problem of sin. It is
a two-fold promise: God promises to forget our sins and rejuvenate our
hearts with his Word (Jesus). When he forgets our sins, he wipes the slate
clean. He washes the stains of sin from our hearts so that we might be
born again through Christ. He also promises to instill our hearts and
minds with his laws. Under the Old Covenant, someone could practice
the faith with a corrupt heart, but the New Covenant cannot be kept
by a corrupt heart. God's complete forgiveness and his claiming of our
hearts and minds means that, as Christians, we are in a perpetual state of
salvation.

Though we continue to sin due to our humanity, God continually forgives
us, and the laws written on our souls remind us of what is right and
good according to the Lord. True believers influenced by God's laws
on their hearts are incorruptible. Salvation is accomplished through
the outpouring of the Holy Spirit and a conversion of the heart and

conscience of the believer to God. The Lord's intervention and continual sanctification allow the shackles of death to fall away; through him, we live out his New Covenant. God continually forgives us, and Jesus eternally intercedes with an unending flow of prayer to the Father on our behalf.

The announcement of the New Covenant signals the end of the Old. As of the arrival of Jesus, the Old Covenant is obsolete and vanishes away. Only God's new promise of forgiveness in Christ and heart-changing love remain.

Reflection:

Do you believe that humans are intrinsically bad or good? How does God's salvation alter both our status before God and our nature?

Week 4

Therefore, brothers, since we have confidence to enter the holy places by the blood of Jesus, by the new and living way that he opened for us through the curtain, that is, through his flesh, and since we have a great priest over the house of God, let us draw near with a true heart in full assurance of faith, with our hearts sprinkled clean from an evil conscience and our bodies washed with clean water.

HEBREWS 10:19-22

Day 22

HOLY PLACES | Read Hebrews 9:1-10

There is a reason we seek to worship God in a dedicated church building and not in another space that could accommodate a congregation and speaker. While we often do it, particularly with new church plants, there is something that doesn't feel quite right to have a worship service in a common space that has not been set aside for worship. Though the New Testament requirements for church services are not as clearly defined as Old Testament Tabernacle worship, most modern churches have a similar look. They all have one essential thing in common: every church is a sacred space dedicated to worship, a facsimile of the house of the Lord God Almighty. We come to the "house of God" to worship him together in harmony.

Through the architecture of modern churches varies widely across the country and across denominations, each church has similar features: pews or chairs for the congregation; a pulpit; an altar or table; a font for baptism; and usually a piano, organ, or keyboard for music. In the days of the Old Covenant, however, the structure of the worship space and the structure of the worship ceremony were clearly specified by God. The instructions for Tabernacle worship were quite detailed and involved many items representative of Israel's history. These remembrances of the intervention of God on Israel's behalf and his covenant with them reminded the priests of God's faithful provision for the needs of his people.

The detailed rituals of the Tabernacle, however, were destined to be inadequate—the people were too far away from God. Only the high priest could enter the Holy of Holies, and no offering he made could ever compensate fully for the sins of the people. No matter how carefully the congregants set up the tent and carried out the rituals, they would never be able to enter the Holy of Holies, for God had ordained only one representative—the high priest—to stand in his presence, only once a year. The other problem with Old Covenant worship was that these rituals could be carried out with a corrupted heart. Because the people had no divine intercessor, they had to rely on human intercession, which will always fall short. The New Covenant changed the focus, placing the emphasis on the sincerity of our hearts in worship of the Lord.

In studying the rituals of worship in the Old and New Covenants, theologians have identified patterns that illuminate our understanding of what it means to partake in a worship service. It's evident that God desires to be approached in a certain way from the commands he issues and the way worship is carried out. In the Old Covenant, God wished to remain totally hidden, offering only one priest a semblance of intimacy behind the curtains. The rituals and accoutrements were detailed and sacred and served as symbols of earthly and heavenly things. In a way, the Old Covenant worship was more externally demonstrative—the priests wore clothing items symbolizing both the honor and guilt of the people, and sacrificed animals in a symbolic appeal for absolution.

With the arrival of the New Covenant, worship changed. Instead of only one person accessing God, any believer can access him through Jesus. There are no more blood sacrifices to be made after Jesus Christ, and there is no more need for the rituals of the Old Covenant. Laws are carried out in the heart. However, there's one similarity: in both covenants, God cannot be accessed directly. It's clear that God desires, even requires, to be approached though a mediator as our hearts will always be spoiled with sin. In the New Covenant, Jesus serves as our perfect mediating intercessor. We approach the Lord only though Jesus' priestly ministry and his cleansing blood.

There is an element of mystery with the Lord of Lords, one that the author of Hebrews acknowledges by holding back details in his sermon. There is a mystery of ritual that only the initiated know, and so the preacher treads lightly lest a non-initiate hear his words. Though the book of Hebrews focuses on the structure and meaning of Christian worship, the preacher never mentions the practical details of holy Communion. Some things must remain sacred for the baptized. He also leaves an element of mystery regarding our intimacy with the Lord, for we can only know God through a conduit, and we can only know him by experience.

God remains a hidden God—it is only through partaking of the holy mysteries of the body and blood of Jesus Christ that we can gain access to the Most Holy Place. Jesus cleanses our hearts of sin so we can interact with the divine and achieve salvation through him. Unlike the people of the Old Covenant, we can enter the Holy of Holies—Jesus has ripped away the old curtain and taken down the dividers erected in the old laws! For those who choose to commit to him, we can have communion with the Triune God covered in the righteousness of his Son.

Reflection:

We live in a world of distraction and often walk into church looking for our friends or scrolling through our phones. When you approach the sanctuary for worship, how do you enter his holy space? When you take communion, how do you approach the table of God, the earthly symbol of his heavenly altar?

Day 23

ATONING BLOOD | Read Hebrews 9:11-14

The Lord requires demonstrative worship through sacrifice. Nowadays, we demonstrate our devotion by tithing part of our earnings and through offering our hearts to Jesus. Like worshipers of old we continue to sacrifice our life and labor as a thanksgiving offering to the Lord. In the Old Covenant, God also required animal sacrifices of goats, bulls, and other livestock. He asked for blood sacrifices. He sets out some of the regulations for these sacrifices in Leviticus 17:3-6:

> *"If any one of the house of Israel kills an ox or a lamb or a goat in the camp, or kills it outside the camp, and does not bring it to the entrance of the tent of meeting to offer it as a gift to the Lord in front of the tabernacle of the Lord, bloodguilt shall be imputed to that man. He has shed blood, and that man shall be cut off from among his people. This is to the end that the people of Israel may bring their sacrifices that they sacrifice in the open field, that they may bring them to the Lord, to the priest at the entrance of the tent of meeting, and sacrifice them as sacrifices of peace offerings to the Lord. And the priest shall throw the blood on the altar of the Lord at the entrance of the tent of meeting and burn the fat for a pleasing aroma to the Lord."*

Blood represented life—every animal had to be bled out before it could be eaten, and the blood was a required offering to the Lord. By offering the blood of slaughtered animals to God, the people were really offering God the life of those animals. It was a way of honoring God, the giver of all life, while also ensuring that their food would be fit for consumption. Wasting the life of an animal was expressly forbidden because to waste one of God's creations would be disrespectful to him. The *"peace offerings"* of blood and fat were also intended to shield the Israelites from God's just wrath, for if they failed to give the sacrifices, they would be thrown out of the camp, excommunicated from God's holy community. However, it wasn't just about staying in the group—this blood was meant as a substitute for human blood since God required sacrifices of appeasment, but forbade human sacrifice. The ancient Israelites believed that the blood of these animals would satiate God's justice.

Unfortunately for the people of the Old Testament, the blood of animals did not satisfy God's holy requirements for justice. Though the blood of animals could purify the flesh, it could not purify the soul, and therefore the ancient Israelites could not enter the kingdom of heaven without a better sacrifice. The blood kept the Israelites from the harshness of God's judgement, but it could not do more than that. But God had plans for a New Covenant that would not require the blood of animals: he sent Jesus to serve as our eternal priest and as the final blood sacrifice. This final sacrifice is what actually saved those in the Old Testament who faithfully followed God—the animal sacrifices were merely a sacramental symbol to them of the future "once and for all" sacrifice that would eternally save their souls, and ours.

The ritual work of the Great High Priest, Jesus, stands in contrast to the work of the Old Covenant priests. Unlike the old order, Jesus does not enter a human sanctuary *"of this creation,"* but instead he entered *"once and for all into the holy places"* (Hebrews 9:11-12). He passes through the earthly copies of the house of God to stand in the Holy of Holies. At the heavenly altar of God, he does not offer the blood of animals. He offers his own life, perfect and without sin, in order to purify the consciences of all who follow him. Christ's blood washes away our sin and dirtiness, our guilt and shame, so that we might serve the Living God without fear and self-hiding.

In the communion ritual, followers partake of the body and blood of Christ. When we eat the bread that symbolizes Christ's flesh and drink the wine that symbolizes his blood, we are consecrated with his sacrifice. His sprinkled blood purifies us to commune with God Almighty. Christ's sacrifice saved humanity from the rigorous and vain slaughter of animals. By opening his veins upon the altar of God, Jesus ensured that there would always be a path to salvation for every human being. Paul writes in Romans 5:8-9, *"God shows his love for us in that while we were still sinners, Christ died for us. Since therefore we have now been justified by his blood, much more shall we be saved by him from the wrath of God.*" When humankind was alienated from God, Jesus died for us so that we might know God intimately.

And so the prophecy of Jeremiah 31 is ultimately accomplished through the blood of Christ: "*I will forgive their iniquity, and I will remember their sins no more*" (Jeremiah 31:34). All transgressions and sins are once and for all washed away. Through the redemption of Christ, we are granted the right as rescued children of God to receive the *promised eternal inheritance*.

Reflection:

The communion ritual involves the transformation of simple things into the holiest sacraments. How can you use your spiritual imagination when taking communion to establish a deeper connection to Christ and his sacrifice?

Day 24

ONCE FOR ALL | Read Hebrews 9:15-28

Long before the earthly death of Jesus Christ, God had a plan for our salvation. Recorded by prophets, the Bible makes it clear that a Savior was fated to offer himself for humanity. The premeditated nature of the New Covenant makes it similar to a last will and testament. Just like a human will, the New Covenant was designed in anticipation of a future event. I have prepared my own will so that if I were to die suddenly, my family would be provided for. But my last will and testament will not be relevant until I pass. Likewise, God made humanity the beneficiaries of his last covenant: we inherit eternal life, but it was contingent on the death of Jesus Christ. When Jesus died on the Cross, offering himself in an act of ultimate sacrifice, we inherited eternal life through him. That is when the New Covenant took effect and voided the Old Covenant.

The preacher to the Hebrews writes, *"Indeed, under the law almost everything is purified with blood, and without the shedding of blood there is no forgiveness of sins"* (Hebrews 9:22). The flesh of those under the Old Covenant was purified with the blood of animals, but the souls of those in the New Covenant are purified with the blood of Jesus. This purification also covers the souls of those in the Old Testament who trusted in God.

The purification properties of blood also extend to promises. The biblical promises of God were made pure and binding with blood as the preacher points out in verses 19-21: *"For when every commandment of the law had been declared by Moses to all the people, he took the blood of calves and goats, with water and scarlet wool and hyssop, and sprinkled both the book and all the people, saying, 'This is the blood of the covenant that God commanded for you.' And in the same way he sprinkled with the blood both the tent and all the vessels used in worship."* Biblical promises are sealed with blood in both the Old Covenant and the new. Jesus' blood served as both the final seal and fulfillment of the New Covenant. With his blood, he opened the gates of salvation to the inheritors of God's promise.

Jesus came to live amongst people for the singular purpose of his eventual sacrificial death. He appeared once for all time to deal with sin. Unlike the sacrifices of the Old Covenant, the sacrifice of Jesus requires no vain repetition. He only did so *once*. We say in our baptism ceremony that the baptized person is buried with Christ in his death and raised with him in new life. One of the reasons why we do not repeat the sacrament of baptism in the life of a believer is because of the connection of baptism with the one-time sacrifice of Jesus. It is once for all. This is why the preacher challenges us to not fall away—we cannot go back to pre-baptism and then repeat the symbol of the one time sacrifice of Jesus, for to do so would go against the terms of God's covenant with us seeking to repeat the unrepeatable. The Book of Common Prayer puts it this way: "…of thy tender mercy didst thou give thine only son, Jesus Christ, to suffer death upon the cross for our redemption; who made there, by his one oblation of himself once offered, a full, perfect, and sufficient sacrifice, oblation, and satisfaction, for the sins of the whole world" (p.334). Jesus will never be re-crucified because he accomplished all that was needed, perfectly, forever.

He gave his life for us once for all time. In the same way, we give our lives to him once for all time. That is not to say that we don't have times of faltering, temptations, or uncertainties. It is to say that the terms of the New Covenant are bound in the life of the believer with the blood of Jesus for eternity. This one-time sprinkling with Christ's blood symbolized by the waters of our baptism purifies the hearts and minds of all initiated into faith in Jesus, forever. As we pronounce to the newly baptized with the anointing oil of Christ, "you are sealed by the Holy Spirit in baptism and marked as Christ's own forever" (BCP, p. 308). The knowledge of our eternal covenant provides the believer with tremendous assurance in times of faltering, temptations, and uncertainties.

Now that Jesus has made the one ultimate and final sacrifice on our behalf, the New Covenant has begun and the continual shedding of blood required by the Old Covenant has drawn to a close. "It is finished!", he cried, as he breathed his last (John 19:30). The preacher to the Hebrews describes the timing of Jesus' arrival as *"at the end of the ages"* (Hebrews 9:26). And indeed, Jesus' arrival and death signaled the most significant transition of history. Not only did God's relationship with humanity transition from the Old Covenant to the New Covenant, but a new historic age began—the last days.

Historians used to commonly use the abbreviation B.C., meaning Before Christ, when referring to the years before Christ's birth. Now, in an attempt to secularize historical terms, they use B.C.E., meaning Before the Common Era. With either abbreviation, it is clear that the birth of Christ was a major turning point in the history of the world. No matter what you call it, Jesus began a new era and new age both historically and spiritually and his death catalyzed the greatest change in God's laws. Jesus ushered in a new age of forgiveness. When we are under the New Covenant and washed in Christ's blood, God will forgive and forget our sins. We are born anew in his grace! As followers of Christ and faithful participants, we inherit not only God's forgiveness but also eternal life through Jesus. In the present era of God's mercy, we need not fear death, for we can rest in the knowledge that we will return to the heart of God.

Though Jesus only died once and will not die again, he is destined to return again. When he appears next, it will not be to die for our sins all over again. His coming appearance will be to save ultimately and finally those who are waiting for him. Our eternal high priest is determined to save us—he has already rescued us from the chains of sin by making the ultimate sacrifice and ensuring God's forgiveness. He will come again to inaugurate a new heavens and new earth where we will live in his presence forever!

Reflection:

Sometimes we are harder on ourselves (and others) than God is. Do you find yourself rehashing old guiltsand shame? How does Jesus' once for all sacrifice help you to stop licking old wounds and rehashing past failings?

Day 25

The old sacrificial system was never able to accomplish the aims of God for his people because the old system could not wash away sin. The blood sacrifices of the Old Testament could never fully please God. If they could, the writer to the Hebrews says, then why would the priests continue to offer sacrifices regularly? They were inadequate. The animal sacrifices served to reveal the human need for cleansing due to our constant sin, but they could not cleanse the people the way God needed. God did not want his people to have only awareness of their sins without having a permanent solution, but that was the reality of the Old Covenant. The law could only judge, so the sacrifices could only deflect that judgement—the law could not forgive.

God wanted his people to draw near, but sin cannot abide in the presence of a Holy, Holy, Holy God. A way was needed to exchange our sinfulness for perfect holiness. Because the Lord desired to commune with us despite our sin, he sent Jesus Christ to act as the perfect and final sacrifice. The ultimate goal of God was to bring us into communion with him; he accomplished this through Jesus. We need not only to be forgiven for our sin, but to be clothed in the righteousness of Jesus—that is the only way to holiness. God desires us to draw near to him in holiness. We are called to move beyond awareness of our sin and move into intimacy with the Lord.

When my children were growing up, my wife and I made a concerted effort to have family dinners. We would sit down with our children after a long day and engage with them over our meal. We talked about our days. We went around the table and shared the best part of our time at school or work—often these highlights were simple things like getting to watch a movie during recess or enjoying a phone call with an old friend. Some evenings we asked one another to describe any kind act we'd witnessed or done, and that gave us an opportunity to develop our children's character.

Just talking over a meal brought us closer together as a family. We grew to understand one another on a deeper level and that shared understanding made it easier to mitigate conflict and get along. We built community in our home around the table.

Often when we hear the word "communion," we think of the ritual we engage in every Sunday. And that is accurate! But the name of this sacred ritual implies much about its meaning. The verb "to commune" means "to receive Holy Communion." But the Oxford English Dictionary offers an additional meaning for this verb: "to share one's intimate thoughts and feelings with someone, especially on a spiritual level." During the sacrament of Holy Communion, we commune with God—over a meal, we share our intimate selves with the Lord.

God's will is togetherness. He wants us to join him at his table so that we can be intimate with him. In fact, he has been preparing his table for us. But without the forgiveness of our sins, we cannot join him. The solution is Christ, who won our forgiveness so that we might join our Father at the table. Jesus knew that the desire of God was not the blood of bulls and goats, but the perfect sacrifice of himself, Jesus the Son, in submission to the Father's will. He says so by quoting Psalm 40 where David sang, "*In sacrifice and offering you have not delighted…Burnt offering and sin offering you have not required. Then I said, 'Behold, I have come; in the scroll of the book it is written of me; I delight to do your will, O my God; your law is within my heart'*" (Psalm 40:6-8).

The coming of the Messiah ushered in a new age of communion and intimacy with the Lord. The old way is finished and done; God has replaced it with a better covenant, for satisfaction of judgement alone did not bring joy to the heart of God. Through Jesus, God has accomplished his desire to bring his people closer to him. We are sanctified by the offering of the body of Jesus Christ! The preacher to the Hebrews writes, "*And by that will we have been sanctified through the offering of Jesus Christ once for all*" (Hebrews 10:10). The blood of Christ has washed us clean. His forgiveness of our sin and imparting to us his righteousness makes us perfect so that we can draw near.

We can now share a meal with God and truly commune with him the way he always wanted.

Linger in your communion with the Lord, for it is his will that you draw close to him in intimate table fellowship.

Reflection:

Do you feel yourself drawing near to God when you take Holy Communion? What keeps you from lingering at his table?

Day 26

It's not easy to be a Christian. Following Jesus all day, every day, can get tiring! In the Old Testament, the priests stood while they made sin offerings over and over all day long. I can't imagine how exhausting that must have been. Day after day, week after week, the priests performed the same rituals. The priests of the Old Testament never got a break because they were bound by law to continue making sacrifices for the sins of the people. Because redemption wasn't yet accomplished, they had to keep up the ritual offerings, even as they grew exhausted.

But Christ offers true redemption, a once and for all salvation that eliminated the need for animal offerings. The ways of the Old Covenant became obsolete with the dawn of a new age of forgiveness. No longer would humanity toil in vain towards an impossible perfection, for God sent his son to die for our sins.

When Christ made the final offering of his body, the writer of Hebrews says, "*He sat down at the right hand of God.*" (Hebrews 10:12). Christ's single sacrifice accomplished what the priests' repeated offerings could not— Jesus redeemed us forever in the eyes of God. That redemption, that cleansing of sin, that complete forgiveness, allowed us to achieve God's will of togetherness. Jesus sits down because his work is finished.

In one offering for all time, Jesus also secured for us the New Covenant gift of the Holy Spirit through which our hearts are perfected. He quotes Jeremiah 31: "'*This is the covenant that I will make with them after those days, declares the Lord: I will put my laws on their hearts, and write them on their minds,*' then he adds, '*I will remember their sins and their lawless deeds no more*'" (Hebrews 10:16-17). Using this verse, Jesus reminds us that the New Covenant brings about a change of heart because of the internal implantation of his law in us. The full forgiveness we have through Christ gives us a clean slate and a pure heart.

My grandfather fought in World War II and continued to work hard all his life. When he retired, he spent long stretches of time sitting at the end of his dock watching the waves, birds, and sunsets. Sometimes he tossed out a fishing line, but mostly he just sat and enjoyed the peaceful environment. He rested in God's creation and took great pleasure in observing it. He had a saying that he repeated often: "Why run when you can walk, and why walk when you can sit?" He had finally reached the part of his life when he could sit instead of walk and he used the time simply to enjoy the glory of God's creation. Through Christ's sacrifice, we too can finally rest in the peace of our salvation.

Now that the great work of redemption is accomplished, Jesus invites us to sit and enjoy God's presence. Jesus sits down on the right hand of God, his work done, and we're invited into the holy peace, the Sabbath Rest that he alone provides. We can relax in the knowledge that, through Christ, we are saved. We celebrate this salvation and sacrifice in one of the Eucharistic Prayers when we say, "Holy and gracious Father: In your infinite love you made us for yourself; and, when we had fallen into sin and become subject to evil and death, you, in your mercy, sent Jesus Christ, your only and eternal Son, to share our human nature, to live and die as one of us, to reconcile us to you, the God and Father of all. He stretched out his arms upon the cross, and offered himself, in obedience to your will, a perfect sacrifice for the whole world." We don't have to justify ourselves to him, and we don't need to work to earn his perfect peace. It is a true gift, offered from a place of utmost love!

Perhaps one of the most gracious parts of Jesus' sacrifice is that it was made once for all. "All" encompasses all people and all time. Paul writes in Romans 10:10-13, *"For with the heart one believes and is justified, and with the mouth one confesses and is saved. For the Scripture says, 'Everyone who believes in him will not be put to shame.' For there is no distinction between Jew and Greek; for the same Lord is Lord of all, bestowing his riches on all who call on him. For 'everyone who calls on the name of the Lord will be saved.'"* The forgiveness of God transcends race, geographic boundaries, time, and prejudices. Truly, Jesus' sacrifice was for every person who desires to know God. As we pray to the Great High Priest, "Lord Jesus Christ, you stretched out your arms of love on the hard wood of the cross that everyone might come within the reach of your saving embrace…"(BCP, p. 101).

Once and for all, we are redeemed through God's merciful gift of forgiveness through Jesus Christ. Hallelujah! What a Savior.

Reflection:

Think back to when you first trusted Jesus as your Savior and truly became his follower. How did the radical forgiveness of Jesus change your life then? How does it influence you now?

Day 27

It is not enough to know *about* Jesus' sacrifice on our behalf. Studying the word of God is an important endeavor, but without actually experiencing the deep forgiveness and peace of the Lord, such knowledge is inadequate. Likewise, it is not enough *to believe* in God without consummating that relationship—as believers in Christ, we must enter into God's presence and commune in his Sabbath Rest.

Here is the central invitation to which the entire book of Hebrews builds: We are exhorted to enter into communion with the Holy Trinity through the sacramental presence of Jesus. Recall the sanctuary curtain in the Tabernacle that barred access to the Holy of Holies. When Jesus died upon the Cross, that curtain was torn apart: Matthew wrote, "*Jesus cried out again with a loud voice and yielded up his spirit. And behold, the curtain of the temple was torn in two, from top to bottom*" (Matthew 27:50-51). Jesus' death destroyed the solid physical barrier between humanity and God even as it destroyed the spiritual barrier of sin.

With the destruction of the physical curtain, there was the creation of a spiritual curtain—the curtain of Jesus' flesh. But unlike the physical curtain of the old Tabernacle, which served to keep people out, the curtain of Jesus' flesh *lets people in* to the presence of God. Jesus' death removed every obstacle between humanity and intimacy with the Lord.

Before Jesus was crucified, he took a last meal with the disciples, during which he demonstrated the first communion. The priest repeats the words he spoke before we participate in the ritual of communion:

> On the night he was handed over to suffering and death, our Lord Jesus Christ took bread; and when he had given thanks to you, he broke it, and gave it to his disciples, and said, 'Take, eat: This is my Body, which is given for you. Do this for the remembrance of

me.' After supper he took the cup of wine; and when he had given thanks, he gave it to them, and said, 'Drink this, all of you: this is my Blood of the New Covenant, which is shed for you and for many for the forgiveness of sins. Whenever you drink it, do this for the remembrance of me."

(BCP P362-3)

When we consume the bread and wine, we pass through the spiritual curtain of Jesus' flesh and enter into the holy realm of the Lord. The mysterious entry beyond the veil is the most intimate moment we have with God while still on Earth; we are called to draw near in full assurance of our faith.

We can stand firm in full assurance because, through Jesus, we have been given true hearts, souls sprinkled clean from an evil conscience, and bodies washed with pure water. We enter the presence of the Lord through the veil of Jesus' flesh and his sacramentally consumed body. As we consume the sacramental body and blood, we enter the Living God.

Though our sacramental entry into the heavenly kingdom takes place during communion, we are called to linger in that holy place and stay intimate with God even after we have left the sanctuary. The preacher to the Hebrews calls for followers of Christ to encourage one another to remain close to God. It's easy to leave the church and go about your week without reaching out to other members of the body of Christ, but we must spur each other on to good works. A lack of intimacy in the body of the church is dangerous.

When individual members fall away, the bonds between all the believers weaken. The best way to remain in the Holy of Holies in the full assurance of your faith is to hold fast to your beliefs, worship regularly, and stay connected to your brothers and sisters in Christ. Stay in communion with one another not only in worship but also in the accountable fellowship of believers throughout the week. This spiritual intimacy with one another in turn strengthens our intimacy with God.

The Prayer After Communion in the Book of Common Prayer echoes the extortion of the Hebrews' writer to continue to live in intimacy with God:

> *Eternal God, heavenly Father, you have graciously accepted us as living members of your Son our Savior Jesus Christ, and you have fed us with spiritual food in the Sacrament of his Body and Blood. Send us now into the world in peace and grant us strength and courage to love and serve you with gladness and singleness of heart; through Christ our Lord. Amen."*

BCP P.365

We have been welcomed into the Holy of Holies, the throne room of God Most High, passing through the veil of Jesus' flesh to enter God's peace. When we commune with God, we fulfill his will for intimacy with his people. Through Jesus, we are made whole, and we must strive to encourage one another to keep the faith.

Reflection:

Think about the people who have encouraged you to keep coming to church every Sunday. Who in your life encourages you to stay intimate with God? How do you encourage your brothers and sisters in Christ to stay firm in their faith?

Day 28

Our modern world is rife with disbelief and doubt. Everything feels as though it's up for debate. This constant barrage of questioning can lead to a dilution of faith for those who are not deliberately following Jesus. Simply put, people take God too lightly and doubt can be contagious. There's a pervasive thought that our individual behavior and actions don't matter in the grand scheme of things, but the reality is that they do matter. When doubt is entertained about the salvation of God, the same doubt falls over the judgement of God and belief in the consequences for our behavior falls away.

For followers of God, abiding in rebelion, disbelief, and doubt are not options. When you choose the path of the Living God, you must stay the course. Communion with the Lord is not a one-time action: it is not a box to check to ensure a ticket to heaven and it is not a commitment to take lightly. Once you commune with God, you cannot slip away from his grace without fear of his wrath. For what is worse, to need forgiveness or to reject it? As humans, we are bound to sin, but Jesus offers us forgiveness. While this forgiveness is eternal, to abuse that mercy is a deep transgression against God. You cannot keep living an earthly lifestyle full of deliberate sin once you commit yourself to God. The writer of Hebrews reminds his audience that to do so means *"there no longer remains a sacrifice for sins, but a fearful expectation of judgement, and a fury of fire that will consume the adversaries"* (Hebrews 10:26-27). To reject God's gift of complete forgiveness is to incur his eternal fury.

This is a warning against willful apostasy. The alternative to intimacy with God is eternal suffering, especially for those who continue to go against the New Covenant once they've entered into it. To break the law of man is one thing, but to break the law of the Lord is another. God offered up Jesus Christ and, through him, gave us eternal salvation and forgiveness. How could we turn away from the abundance of mercy that he has offered us? To turn away from such grace once we've received it profanes his gift. It insults him, and when angered, God will not hesitate to punish transgressors with his full wrath. These verses in Hebrews are a dire warning of what will come to pass for those who act against God.

But take heart: God does not want to punish his children! He isn't waiting for you to mess up; it's simply that the Lord does not like to be taken for granted. Consider the way spoiled children treat their parents. They don't think about the laundry, cooking, cleaning, and other work that goes into giving them a nice home. They don't take care of the clothes and toys their parents provide—they just expect to be given new ones when they ruin the old. Often in these situations, there's a tipping point where a child will feel so entitled that the parent will finally express his or her anger and in frustration punish the child for the ungrateful behavior.

Another example is that of spouses. Sometimes one spouse goes out of the way to provide for the other, whether it's cooking meals, providing financial security, or offering constant emotional support. When the other one takes their spouse's care for granted without giving much in return, there's tension in the marriage. But when it reaches the point where one spouse feels entitled to the point that they do not think of their spouse and act deceitfully or cheat, there are severe consequences. Often, a transgression against the sanctity of a marriage will result in the end of the relationship. That is what the writer to the Hebrews is trying to convey—if you willfully rebel against God and profane the relationship in rebellion or ingratitude to the point where it cannot be mended, you will lose the relationship all together.

It is often those closest to use that we take for granted. We need to be careful that we don't get close enough to the line of irreparable damage of the relationship that we're in danger of crossing it. The same is even truer of our relationship with God. A Christian shouldn't walk around with a sense of condemnation—you have been forgiven in Christ! —but if you deliberately keep sinning by living an earthly lifestyle, do not forget that you may move from a position of assured salvation to most certain judgement. We cannot take grace for granted, and we should fear a life away from God, for a life estranged from God is death.

So how can we avoid drifting so far that we lose God? We must reject sin completely! We must deflect doubt and disbelief with a shield of God's word—God always keeps his promises, and we must stand firm in that knowledge. To doubt is natural—God doesn't' condemn our doubt. But he asks us to do as "doubting Thomas" did—bring our doubt and uncertainty to the Savior. We can and should ask Jesus for help in overcoming our lack of belief. And while our thoughts and emotions may linger in a state of doubt for a time, we can still continue to walk in obedience to the Lord. In fact, faith often follows action. Eventually, if we seek the Lord's help in times of doubt, we will emerge with even stronger faith in the salvation of Jesus Christ.

Salvation comes to those who persevere with the saints. There must be progress in our relationship with God. We need to always be going forward. As Christians, we are called to keep our intimacy with God alive and draw close to him each day. If we slip away, let us return quickly. We will continue to fall into sin as long as we are on this earth. But when we sin, we need to go to God right away, confess, ask forgiveness, and repent (turn in the other direction.) For to continue unrepentant in sin is to trade our assurance of salvation for a fearful dread of judgement.

Reflection:

Consider your lifestyle, doubts, fears, and questions. Is your salvation in jeopardy? How can you quell the rebelliousness in your heart?

Week 5

TRUSTING IN THINGS PROMISED YET UNSEEN

Therefore, since we are surrounded by so great a cloud of witnesses, let us also lay aside every weight, and sin which clings so closely, and let us run with endurance the race that is set before us, looking to Jesus, the founder and perfecter of our faith, who for the joy that was set before him endured the cross, despising the shame, and is seated at the right hand of the throne of God.

HEBREWS 12:1-2

Day 29

A HARD STRUGGLE | Read Hebrews 10:32-39

Members of the early Church endured many contests and struggles of suffering. They were made a public spectacle, berated with insults, and faced persecution. Yet, they stood in solidarity with their brothers and sisters in Christ in prison and strived to joyfully bear the plundering of their property.

How did they get through such loss? By continually reminding themselves of God's promise of a better possession. Their faith was strengthened by the courage and confidence required of them in trials. When we aren't forced to stand strong publicly for the faith, it's actually easier to fall away. It can be a greater challenge to hold fast to Christ in times of blessing and abundance than in times of persecution. The preacher reminds his readers how they survived tough times with boldness and joy in order to encourage them to stand firm for the long haul, during easier times when the struggle and burden seem lighter.

The Lord's aim is that we stay connected to him though the best and worst of times. Do not shrink back from communion and intimacy with the Lord. Earlier, the preacher had exhorted:

> *Let us hold fast the confession of our hope without wavering, for he who promised is faithful. And let us consider how to stir up one another to love and good works, not neglecting to meet together, as is the habit of some, but encouraging one another, and all the more as you see the Day drawing near.*

HEBREWS 10:23-25

The key to staying connected to the Lord is faith—have faith and preserve your soul. But the ground of our faith is not ourselves, but the faithfulness of God in Jesus Christ. Up to this point in the book of Hebrews, whenever faith is mentioned, it is always in reference to the faithfulness of God to us through Jesus Christ. We hold fast *"because he who has promised is faithful"* (Hebrews 10:23). We were also challenged to consider the faithfulness of Jesus in Hebrews 2:17, when he is described as *"a merciful and faithful high priest in the service of God."* Jesus' faithfulness included taking on frail flesh and blood in order that he might sympathize with us in our weakness and sufferings. He is the One who can help us in our weakness, *"if we will draw near to him"* (Hebrews 4:12).

We live in a sinful and fallen world. Living as a Christian in such a hostile environment involves struggle and suffering. Being a Christian is no longer cool—it is not cool in our schools or our workplaces. Christians are often seen as ignorant and stubborn enemies to progress. They are shamed into silence in schools and universities when they insist on the centrality of God. They are quieted into submission in the workplace because expressions of faith are considered inappropriate and offensive to others. In social settings, Christians pursuing holiness of life are considered out of touch and out of place by those reveling in the depravity of our world.

The writer to the Hebrews is reminding his readers of the persecutions they and earlier Christians faced to inspire them to hold fast. He describes their plight as a *"hard struggle with sufferings"* (Hebrews 10:32). But now, that persecution had subsided. They were getting back to "life as usual." And "life as usual" meant the danger of slipping back into pre-conversion patterns and a worldly way of living.

Have you noticed in your own life that it can be easier to be a person of faith, hope, and love when you're going through a time of persecution than it is during times of peace? In times of plenty, it is easy to take the Lord and his people for granted and to gradually slip away.

I remember after 9/11, churches were packed. The entire Congress of the United States—Democrats and Republicans—came out on the steps of the Capitol together and sang *God Bless America*. So much of our nation was united in seeking the Lord's peace in that crisis. But after the months went by—it didn't take long—people slipped back into ordinary

life again, often without thought of God. The wakeup call had come with suffering but ended soon after.

What kind of persecutions have you endured that awakened your need for God? What kind of sufferings have you gone through that brought you closer to the Lord? Have there been times in your life when you drifted away? What do you think was going on with you in respect to your circumstances?

We need to be reminded of our past faithfulness during struggles and draw from those memories to find strength for the now. The faith and trust the Hebrew Christians had in days of persecution, says the preacher, can serve as a foundation for vigorous faith now. But he is worried about their faltering. He is concerned that they are shrinking back and falling away under lesser pressures.

Beware when you find it easy to take God for granted. As you get older and older, and the years go by, do not lose heart and become discouraged. As you see the schisms in the Church over cultural, social, racial, and political agendas and the corruption in Church leadership, it can be easy to get disheartened. When you witness friends falling away, giving up on engagement with the church, and returning to a worldly lifestyle, it may be tempting to do the same thing. The questions can haunt us: Why am I still hanging on? Why do I continue to worship every week? Why am I still doing this Christian work? Why do I keep shepherding these sheep who are biting me?

It's hard. It's hard to hang in there with the Church over the years. When you have been part of it for 20, 30, 40, 50 years or more, you've "been there, done that" and it can be a challenge to keep on.

The reminder of the book of Hebrews is that there is an end to the challenge, the trials, and the tribulations! There will be a day when the biting sheep stop biting:

"For yet 'in a very little while,
  the one who is coming will come and will not delay;
  but my righteous one will live by faith.
  My soul takes no pleasure in anyone who shrinks back'"

HEBREWS 10:38, NRSV

So what the writer of Hebrews is challenging us to have is *faith*. To hang in there with God's promises, to believe them and to trust in what Jesus did for us and the grace he gives us now. If you are in a place of faithful intimacy, great! Stay connected to the Lord. Stay in that intimate holy place. Guard your life in his holiness and maintain accountable fellowship with other Christians; you will not shrink back or fall away.

Reflection:

Are you in a posture of deliberate sinning? Have you fallen out of the habit of regular worship? Have you allowed discouragement over an apathetic church to make you apathetic about Christ? Know that God delights in the steadfast! If you feel like throwing in the towel, remind yourself that God wants to help you endure and persevere. Our faithfulness is a sign of Christ's faithfulness being perfected in us. When you are tempted to slip away, allow the warnings of the preacher to spur you to repentance. Such back sliding is not characteristic of believers, he says: *"But we are not among those who shrink back and so are lost, but among those who have faith and so are saved"* (Hebrews 10:39 NRSV).
Keep on keeping on!

Persecution

One of the early Christian sufferings was public reproach and affliction because of their faith.

In the Middle East today, the Arabic letter "N" is written on houses to publicly identify the home of a Christian, urging others to shun those who live here in both business and personal life. Those inside are marked for persecution, imprisonment, and even martyrdom. In Iraq, Syria, and other nations in the Middle East, Christians are being dragged from their homes, their sons forced into slavery as boy soldiers and their daughters as child brides.

During the writing of Hebrews, similar events were taking place. Christians were being dragged from their homes, brought before courts, publicly shamed, and accused of all kinds of egregious acts. The preacher says to the reader, not only have some of you been through such trials, but you (at your own risk) have stood as public and empathetic partners with other Christians suffering such reproach. The temptation is to disavow relationships and allow others to suffer alone in an act of self-protection and preservation. But he encourages them, you went through the trial alongside the people you love—family members, friends, fellow church members, and others who faced public shaming. You stood firm and stayed in connection even with those in prison.

He is not simply talking about people in prison in general, but Christians who have been imprisoned for their faith. The early Church stayed connected and had compassion on them and ministered to them. It is very easy for us on the outside, secure, to go on with life and forget about our imprisoned brothers and sisters in Christ who are struggling.

Day 30

To the writer of Hebrews, faith is the key antidote to what is ailing the Church. For those shrinking back from intimacy with the Lord, failing to make public bold confessions, and breaking their commitment to community with one another, he urges greater faith! For an entire chapter, the preacher provides example after example of people of God who faced similar challenges to the Hebrews church and yet stood fast, upholding their faith in God. Hebrews 11 is often called "The Great Hall of Faith" or the "Litany of the Faithful."

The Early Church fathers speak of three types of faith in God:
Credere Deum ("to believe that God is"): This is simply to believe that God exists. This kind of belief has no moral assent. James says, "*even the demons believe in God—and shudder!*" (James 2:19).

Credere Deo ("to believe toward God"): This is a faith that assents to the moral superiority of God and the trustworthiness of his word. If God says of Jesus, "*This is my Son, listen to him,*" a person with this kind of faith believes it (Luke 9:35). If the promises say that Christ died for our sins to forgive us, this faith believes that his word of promise is true and trustworthy.

Credere in Deum ("to believe into God"): This phrase is more difficult to translate, but it is a faith of total reliance on and in God, where the person who has faith literally rests in God. This is placing yourself *into God.* This is the highest goal of faith.

The preacher is encouraging his listeners to have all three levels of faith. In fact, it is impossible to be approved by God and credited as righteous without all three:

And without faith it is impossible to please God, for whoever would approach him must believe that he exists and that he rewards those who seek him. (Hebrews 11:6)

We must *"believe that he exists."* This is *Credere Deum*, the belief that God is. God revealed himself to Moses in the name YHWH, *"I am that I am."* God is the God who is. As the preacher argues in the first chapter of Hebrews, this is the basic assumption of the Christian faith. God is there. When polled, the vast majority of people (usually around 90%) affirms this type of faith in God. [1] But James warns that even devils have this kind of faith. Thus, the limitation of this type of faith is that it is not a faith that will save you. It is essential to believe that God exists, yet it is insufficient for salvation.

Saving faith not only believes that God is, but also believes that God's promises are good and true (*Credere Deo*). As expressed in Hebrews 1, God has continually revealed himself in various ways at various times; but in these last days, God has spoken definitively and supremely through his Son. The Son who also bears the name of YWHW, Jesus, or Yeshua, meaning "the God who is, saves." God doesn't just exist, he also speaks to us and makes promises and covenants. Christian faith is a belief that God *"rewards those who seek him"* (Hebrews 11:6). His promises are true and trustworthy. We are called to believe toward God, to submit to his revelation and trust it. This type of faith is essential as well, but the writer commends the heroes of the faith for exhibiting the third level of faith.

Here is a faith *(Credere in Deum)* that relies on God's promises, even to the point of suffering and death. This faith has a weightiness to it.

I use the simple example of a chair to illustrate the three types of faith. I ask, "Do you believe that there is a chair?" The one who says "yes" has a *Credere Deum* kind of faith—belief that the chair exists. Next I ask, "Do you believe that the chair would bear your weight?" If you say "yes," you have C*redere Deo* faith—belief in the promise the chair makes, to hold you up. Finally I ask, "Will you sit in the chair?" If you do so, you are exhibiting *Credere in Deum* faith.

This is a faith that does not merely give assent to the existence of the chair and believe in the promise of its sturdiness—this is the faith that sits

[1] http://www.gallup.com/poll/147887/Americans-Continue-Believe-God.aspx

in the chair and relies on it with one's whole personhood.

The writer of Hebrews describes faith as *"the assurance of things hoped for, the conviction of things not seen"* (Hebrews 11:1). What assurance of things "hoped for" does the New Covenant Christian need? What are the things "not seen?" Well, much of what the preacher has been talking about are realities "not seen"—better promises, a greater sacrifice, an eternal high priest, and access to the heavenly sanctuary through the body and blood of Christ. We embrace these realities by faith. We trust that they are better possessions than the ones being plundered by persecution.

Faith in God—faith that God exists and that he rewards those who seek him. Faith like Abraham and Noah. Faith to obey even when the calling of God "to do" and "to go" is unclear. Faith to do for the Lord even when you don't fully understand why you are doing it. Faith to go when you do not see fully where you are going or even how to get there. The faith that the preacher commends is one that puts all of one's life on the line for God. It is a call to follow him in the path of faithfulness.

Ultimately, faith is absolute assurance that even if challenge and suffering leads to death, nothing will separate us from the love of God (Romans 8). The examples of Abel and Enoch are those who with resurrection faith. Abel willingly sacrificed his best and first to God knowing that God's promises of resurrection are true; though he died, he received his reward—and through his faith, he still speaks. The testimony of Enoch is one of resurrection by faith.

Indeed, the testimony of all the saints of old is that the reward of our faith now is the gift of eternal life with Our Lord forever.

Reflection:

Do you have faith? How does it inform you decisions? Does your faith address your fears and concerns? Does faith enable you to sacrifice your first and best for God?

Since faith defines a life based on what is not seen rather than what is seen, it thereby also becomes a 'proof'—in the very lives of the humans who live by it—of the reality of the unseen.[2]

LUKE TIMOTHY JOHNSTON

John Gibson Patton

John Gibson Patton was a young Christian missionary to the natives of the New Hebrides Islands in the South Pacific. As he was raising support for this most dangerous call, many in the crowd expressed concern that he was engaged in a foolish endeavor. One old man exclaimed, "The cannibals! You will be eaten by cannibals!"

The young missionary replied, "Mr. Dixon, you are advanced in years now and your own prospect is soon to be laid in the grave, there to be eaten by worms. I confess to you that if I can but live and die serving and honoring the Lord Jesus, it will make no difference to me whether my body is eaten by cannibals or by worms."[3]

Truly, John Gibson Patton had great faith in God's existence and in his commands and promises! But that faith would be tested to the extreme as Patton buried with his own hands his young wife and new baby after they fell prey to disease.

"Let those," he wrote, "who have ever passed through similar darkness, as of midnight, feel for me. I was stunned, and my reason seemed almost to give way. I built a wall of coral round the grave and covered the top with beautiful white coral, broken small as gravel; that spot became my sacred and much-frequented shrine during all the years that, amidst difficulties,

[2]Johnston, Hebrews: A Commentary (Westminster John Knox Press, Louisville, KY 2006, p. 290)

[3]http://wholesomewords.org/missions/biopaton.html copied from Heroes of Faith on Pioneer Trails by E. Myers Harrison. Published by Moody Chicago, Illinois, ©1945.

REV D: JOHN G. PATON

dangers, and deaths, I labored for the salvation of these savage islanders."[4]

Endurance through the struggle proves the reality of the third type of faith—that of full confidence and reliance on God and his promises.

Patton set out to translate the word of God into the language of the natives. As he began translating the Gospel of John, he quickly realized that the tribe lacked a word for "faith" or "believe." These islanders were cannibals. They didn't trust anyone—so much so that they actually lacked a word for "faith" or "trust."

Patton, in a moment of inspiration, rocked back in a chair lifting his feet off the ground. He asked them, "How would you describe what I am doing?" One tribesman offered him a phrase that was the equivalent of "resting one's whole weight on the chair." That is the word Patton used to translate belief and faith: "to rest one's whole weight" on Jesus.

> God so loved the world that whosoever "rests one's own weight" on him shall not perish but have everlasting life.

JOHN 3:16, PARAPHRASED

[4]Ibid.

Day 31

The difference between Christianity and all other belief systems is that Christianity offers salvation. Consider that other belief systems offer enlightenment, a rule of life, and often a system of reward and punishment for good and bad works. Christianity alone offers the promise of a "Great Salvation" for those who trust in the great Savior, Jesus Christ.

The offer of salvation presumes that there is a great danger from which we need saving. The testimony of Scripture is that the danger is actually a future accountability to the Almighty God.

Noah is a great example of a man of faith who believed God and his warnings of future judgement even though everyone else in the world was living according to a different understanding. Truth is truth, even if everyone else in the world ignores it. Noah heard the warning that God would destroy the world by a great flood. By faith, Noah took seriously those warnings. The entirety of humanity had become corrupt; the orientation of their lives was such that they refused to heed the warnings of an imminent judgement.

Jesus describes the state of affairs then and in the future:

> *For as the days of Noah were, so will be the coming of the Son of Man. For as in those days before the flood they were eating and drinking, marrying and giving in marriage, until the day Noah entered the ark, and they knew nothing until the flood came and swept them all away, so too will be the coming of the Son of Man.*

MATTHEW 24:37-39

The promise of the Messiah's second coming raises a similar alarm of pending judgement for humanity. Jesus describes his coming return as a day, not unlike that of the day of Noah, when the entirety of humanity will be judged by God.

This means we have our own opportunity to trust in the warnings of God. Jesus describes the world around us as ignoring the threats of ultimate accountability and final judgment. People are oblivious as they go about living their lives *"eating and drinking, marrying and giving in marriage"* as if there is no sense of urgency or cause for concern. Noah did not manifest an ignorant apathy toward God. Rather, he was a person who put faith into action. He built an ark and thereby saved his family and the future line of humanity.

Noah believed in the yet unseen future fulfillment of God's promise. His respect for God's word translated into radical, faithful action. The preacher of Hebrews commends Noah as an example of faith in action. His ark building not only *"saved his household"* and preserved the human race by extension, it also *"condemned the world"* in its rebellion. The righteous will live by faith. Noah is *"an heir to the righteousness that is in accordance with faith"* (Hebrews 11:7).

Have you ever noticed that when a person lives for God among a crowd that does not, inevitably that person will be challenged and even ridiculed for their different choice? Part of the challenge of living in faith is the having the courage to overcome the pressure of the crowd. You have to be okay with being a fool for Jesus Christ; you have to be comfortable not being understood. You should not be surprised when you are derided for not going along with a worldly lifestyle or worldly way of thinking.

Abraham's Faith in Future Blessings—the Heavenly Homeland

If Noah respected the warnings of promised judgement, Abraham had faith in the promise of future provision, blessing, and reward.

One of the most challenging aspects of faith is believing in the reality of

God and his kingdom in the midst of a culture that does not accept or believe the same things. Those with faith have a citizenship in a promised homeland not of this world. They see themselves as strangers and exiles on the earth. They trust in the promise of something greater—a heavenly country, the city of God.

Abraham was willing to forgo known environments, his existing homeland, and earthly treasures in order to pursue the greater promise of God for himself and his family. The faith of Abraham led him to travel to countries unknown to him, such as Egypt and the land of Canaan, in belief in the promise of future blessings and protection. Such promises may have sounded too good to be true, yet he followed the call of God.

Abraham relinquished the comfort of his earthly home to live in a tent because he saw the offer of God as a much greater inheritance. A tent is a temporary dwelling place. It can be set up and taken down with ease. It is the home of a sojourner. Can we see that everything in this world is of the same nature as a tent? The stuff of this world is temporary; all of it can be set up and taken down. We are sojourners. *"For he looked forward to the city that has foundations, whose architect and builder is God"* (Hebrews 11:10).

By faith, Abraham obeyed when he was called to leave the security of a place he knew. The preacher puts it this way: *"And he went out, not knowing where he was going"* (Hebrews 11:8). He went to live in the Land of Promise, as in a foreign land. So faith is more than just belief in the existence of God, though that's a critical component. It's also a faith that translates into action. It's faith that has legs.

For us, it's faith that moves us in the service of worship. It's faith that draws us near to the Throne of Grace. It's faith that holds the Christian community together even in the face of challenge, temptation, suffering, and ridicule.

Abraham also had faith that extended beyond himself. He trusted in a plan of God that would be realized beyond his own life span. Abraham would never see the day when his descendants would be a great nation, as numerous as the stars. But, because he believed in a God who transcends time and space, he took steps to put that plan into action. He believed there was more—a bigger picture, beyond but not excluding the minutia of everyday life.

So many people ask, "Is there more to life than this?" As they go through their daily lives, focused on raising kids, building a career, accumulating wealth for retirement, and fighting for a better quality of life all along, they often feel something is lacking. They desire a deeper meaning. How do we discover the deeper meaning of our lives? By identifying our lives within the larger story—God's story.

The patriarchs of the Bible—Abraham, Isaac, and Jacob—saw the bigger picture with spiritual eyes. They understood, however limited, that the story of their lives played a significant role in a much larger story of redemptive history. Belief in the grand plan of God shaped the actions of their lives.

Indeed, there is so much more to our story than what we see reflected in the here and now. God is engaging you in an epic journey to an amazing Promised City of blessing and abundance. This world is not your home; you were made for more than this! Will you travel the journey by faith with Abraham, Isaac, and Jacob to the city that has foundations, whose architect and builder is God?

Reflection:

How has God placed his call on your life to think, act, and do for him? How does your faith change the way you live so you're not just living as a secular-minded, worldly person?

Day 32

FAITH WILLING TO SACRIFICE | Read Hebrews 11:17-28

Sometimes the Lord asks us to give things up for him.

Abraham and Sarah had no children. Sarah was beyond the age of childbearing; yet, God promised them a son and, by faith, Abraham believed God. The birth of Isaac was a miraculous intervention in Sarah and Abraham's life. Sarah's pregnancy was also a direct fulfillment of God's promise to give them an heir through whom all God's other promises would be realized—including the blessing of the whole world.

So when the call came from God to sacrifice that very child, it would have made no sense. Yet Abraham obeyed. His faith allowed him to obey a command that surpassed his own understanding.

What was on Abraham's lips as he climbed the mountain of sacrifice with his son may very well have paralleled the lyrics of the Don Moen song:

> "God will make a way
> Where there seems to be no way
> He works in ways we cannot see
> He will make a way for me"

GOD WILL MAKE A WAY, BY DON MOEN

By faith, Abraham offered up Isaac. The preacher writes:

> *"He who had received the promises was ready to offer up his only son, of whom he had been told, 'It is through Isaac that descendants shall be named for you.' He considered the fact that God is able even to raise someone from the dead—and figuratively speaking, he did receive him back."*

HEBREWS 12:17-19

The Genesis story does not explicitly say anything about Abraham's belief in the resurrection. But the fact that Abraham believed God's promise that a future nation would be realized through Isaac *and still* raised the knife against him, indicates he believed God could resurrect his son. Paul says something similar in his letter to the Romans. He writes that Abraham believed in the one *"who gives life to the dead and calls into existence the things that do not exist"* (Romans 4:17). God had given life to a dead womb. He certainly could give life to a dead son.

The provision of the lamb in the thicket as a substitutionary sacrifice would be the "way when there seemed to be no way." Similarly, God's provides his only son, Jesus, who sacrifices himself once for all. He is the way when there seems to be no way. Isaac's return to his father is a resurrection of sorts, as the substitution of the lamb for the son gave life where death reigned.

Moses' Willingness to Suffer Reproach

Moses' parents exercised sacrificial faith when they placed their beautiful son into the waters and trusted in the provision of God. As Moses grew, he sacrificed his own prestige and position as a son of Pharaoh's daughter, *"choosing rather to share ill-treatment with the people of God than to enjoy the fleeting pleasures of sin. He considered abuse suffered for the Christ to be greater wealth than the treasures of Egypt, for he was looking ahead to the reward"* (Hebrews 11:25, RSV).

Moses renounced position, wealth, and pleasure. He gave up a place in Pharaoh's palace. He risked ill-treatment and even death for the sake of the coming Messiah and the reward of God's Kingdom. Is there anything in your life that you would not forsake for Jesus? The faith of Abraham and Moses is one that manifests in a willingness to sacrifice.

In our day and in our nation, Christians have much wealth, tremendous influence, and position. Yet, do we see the same level of sacrifice as those who have less around the world? Sacrifice requires faith.

But the fear of loss and the threat of personal risk are often huge barriers to sacrifice for modern-day Christians.

Where do you see places in your life where risk is hindering you from taking greater steps in obedience to the Lord's call? What are you afraid of losing?

Moses was looking forward to the reward and willingly left all comforts behind to take his path with God and the people of Israel. Could you forsake the wealth and comfort of a king's palace? Could you choose a very tough existence in desert wilderness and wandering, never again to experience worldly riches?

Those who reject the kingdoms of this world, like Moses, forgo not only inherited wealth and blessing from the powers of this world, but they also risk suffering reproach. Could you bear that reproach?

The faithful of old faced the same challenges and temptations we face today. Sadly, many Christians in our day choose the world over Christ's Kingdom. Their commitment to Jesus will only go so far. Ask them to part with money, time, or creature comforts, and they will shrink back from the call of even the most basic invitation to spread of the Gospel in our day.

Yet, there are other followers of Jesus who give tirelessly teaching Sunday school, visiting the imprisoned, comforting the elderly. They weekly serve the lowly, giving up their time, possessions, and even opportunities for higher position in order to be faithful to the call. Which are you? Friend, faith overcomes temptation and fear! Ask God for more faith today to help you endure hardship and accept sacrifice for the sake of the Gospel.

Reflection:

What are the temptations, intimidations, and fears that Christians faced in the days of the Early Church? Are they different or the same as in our day? How so? Can you think of examples where you have sacrificed for the sake of Jesus?

Day 33

Jesus taught that with faith as small as a mustard seed, we can move mountains. The testimony of many Israelite of old is one of mountain-moving faith.

The crossing of the Red Sea is a great example. Here, we see powerful corporate faith in action—faith on the part of the entire nation of Israel. A look back at the story in Exodus reveals that it was a complicated trial of faith.

In Exodus 14, we see the Israelites pinned between two formidable and opposing forces. In front, an impassable body of water. Behind, the pounding hooves of the Egyptian army, unbeatable in strength. With no hope of escape or possible victory in battle, the situation looked hopeless. Defeat was certain.

Fear spread through the masses quickly:

> They said to Moses, 'Is it because there are no graves in Egypt that you have taken us away to die in the wilderness? What have you done to us in bringing us out of Egypt? Is not this what we said to you in Egypt: 'Leave us alone that we may serve the Egyptians'? For it would have been better for us to serve the Egyptians than to die in the wilderness.'"

EXODUS 14:11-12

Moses was confronted with a critical test of leadership in the face of insurmountable odds. He stood between his own opposing forces. On the one side, he was following the Lord by faith; on the other, he was leading a people who were paralyzed by insecurity and fear. Would the fear of the Israelites or the promises of the Lord prevail in Moses mind? Any leader can relate to the difficult position in which Moses stood.

I often look back at my time in ministry to seemingly impossible circumstances in which the Lord provided an unforeseen way forward. For example, several years ago we hired an organist/choir director to lead our traditional music during worship. The only challenge was, we lacked an organ for him to play! We had an electronic keyboard, but it only made use of half his capacity as a musician. By faith, one of our parishioners started a fund to collect donations for a church organ. She started the fund with $100. An organ for our space would be at least $60,000! I almost didn't accept the small donation—why even bother? Within a month of the organ fund's establishment, I received an email offering a free Allen church organ to a good home—a church on the other side of town no longer needed it. The only stipulation was that we would have to pick it up. We used the $100 in the organ fund to move it to our sanctuary!

Moses stood firm in confidence that the Lord would resolve his predicament:

> "But Moses said to the people, "Do not be afraid, stand firm, and see the deliverance that the Lord will accomplish for you today; for the Egyptians whom you see today you shall never see again. The Lord will fight for you, and you have only to keep still."

HEBREWS 14:13-14, NRSV

And so by faith, the Israelites *"passed through the Red Sea as if it were dry land, but when the Egyptians attempted to do so they were drowned"* (Hebrews 11:29, NRSV). What are the insurmountable challenges you face in your life? Perhaps they are dreams and visions from the Lord in which he has called you to do something great for him, but you simply cannot see a way to accomplish it.

Martyrs for Jesus[5]

The Old Testament contains numerous stories of insurmountable obstacles being overcome by the faith of men and women,

---

[5]Parts of this section are adapted and edited from a foreword that I wrote for F. Scott Brown, Out of the Valley: One Man's Stand Against Darkness (Lake Mary, Florida: Creation House, 2008), Used by permission.

including the stories of:

> *"Gideon, Barak, Samson, Jephthah, of David and Samuel and the prophets—who through faith conquered kingdoms, administered justice, obtained promises, shut the mouths of lions, quenched raging fire, escaped the edge of the sword, won strength out of weakness, became mighty in war, put foreign armies to flight. Women received their dead by resurrection."*

HEBREWS 11: 32-35A, NRSV

Yet not every faithful leader sees worldly victory and earthly success by the powerful hand of God. The preacher concludes his great hall of faith with a list of those who paid the ultimate price for faithfulness— endurance to the very end:

> *Others were tortured, refusing to accept release, in order to obtain a better resurrection. Others suffered mocking and flogging, and even chains and imprisonment. They were stoned to death, they were sawn in two, they were killed by the sword; they went about in skins of sheep and goats, destitute, persecuted, tormented— of whom the world was not worthy. They wandered in deserts and mountains, and in caves and holes in the ground.*

HEBREWS 11:35B-38

The systems and powers of this world are marshaled against the people of God. Manifesting faith in a sinful and fallen world is risky. It can get you killed. A man like Job, who had lost everything and was now facing his own death, saw a vision of the risen Lord, *"I know that my redeemer lives and that at the last I will stand upon the earth"* (Job 19:35). There is a *"better resurrection"* held out for those who suffer or die for their faith in Jesus.

The history of the people of God is peppered with the martyrdom of great men and women who saw a better future for their people or understood a fuller revelation of God than those around them. One such biblical figure was the first deacon of the Church, Stephen. As he was being stoned for his faith in Christ, he asked those executing him, *"Which of the prophets did you not stone?"* (Acts 7:52).

There are many heroes today who are committed to doing the right thing in various spheres of our society. Such people are the great lights of our race. Thank God there are such souls of integrity who take a stand for what is right.

Unfortunately, history betrays and reveals our true nature with respect to heroes of the faith and reformers of society. Far too often they are attacked and even destroyed by the human systems they've been ordained by God to reform.

In order to reform mediocrity or uphold truth, one must be willing to stand with a stern will; but even the strongest of wills cannot carry a body through the fires of persecution or the assassin's bullet, such as the one that ended the life of Martin Luther King, Jr. In the words of the hymn *A Mighty Fortress Is Our God*, "*this world with devils filled*," seems to win, overcoming good with evil. Sometimes the forces aligned against change break the reformer. Sometimes the man or woman of faith ends the crusade not with earthly victory, but with martyrdom: *Which of the prophets did you not stone?*

Yet, even such seeming tragedy is not outside God's sovereignty. Mysteriously, he uses our weakness, persecutions, sufferings, failings, and even death to accomplish his plan. Consider the cross of Jesus. Our Savior and Lord was perfected in weakness and suffering. By faith, so shall we be.

Reflection:

What kind of worldly opposition have you faced in your faith? Which Christian martyrs inspire you when you feel the persecution of the world shaking you?

National Day of Prayer

On November 4, 1979, the US Embassy in Tehran, Iran, was compromised and sixty-six Americans were taken hostage. The crisis took place just prior to the election of President Ronald Reagan. Susan Wagner had served in U.S. Embassies overseas and related to the crisis personally. She also knew one of the hostages from her time in service. The Lord placed on her heart a desire for a National Day of Prayer to show support for the families of the hostages and their captive loved ones as well as to seek deliverance for the prisoners by the hand of God. Such an idea may seem crazy. How could one person call an entire nation to prayer? But, by faith, she shared the idea with a neighbor who had been a Christian missionary and an international negotiator for the United States. She writes of the encounter:

> I [was] sure that he would pat me on the head and tell me to continue my prayers. After all, why would the Lord call me to this type of action? I was the person who had, in certain ways, in the previous years turned away from the Lord, had broken my marriage vows, and was struggling to find my way to the future...I was not a church leader nor charged in any way theologically to provide any sort of public leadership."[6]

Yet the neighbor and the Lord took Susan's faith seriously. The neighbor challenged her to share the idea with her minister. Her minister challenged her to address the congregation with the idea the next Sunday. Unbeknownst to Susan, the head of the National Council of Churches happened to be worshiping at her church that morning. Following the service, he handed Susan his card and told her that he would be happy to work with her.

Within 48 hours, a prompting from the Lord was given the platform to become reality. Susan was a willing Christian who followed the voice of the Lord in small steps of faith. Within days, she was put in touch with national faith leaders and a great movement of the Lord was begun.

[6]Wagner, Susan Loved Through the Pain, (Not Yet Published) p. 105.

As the plans took shape, notable celebrities such as Bob Hope and Pat Boone lent their voices to radio spots calling the nation to prayer. The plan was set in place by the first of December. That January 29, 1980, would be called the National Day of Thanksgiving for the Return of the Hostages—this before there was any hint of their release.

On January 20, the day of President Ronald Reagan's inauguration, word came that the hostages were being released. The resolution of Congress establishing January 29 as a National Day of Thanksgiving for the Safe Return of the Hostages became Public Law #1—the first law signed by the newly elected president of the United States.

Susan reflects on the experience, "Millions gave thanks to God on that day that we were a United States of America, that God had answered our prayers, and that the hostages were safe. And I thanked the Lord for that still small voice over Thanksgiving, which had turned into a phenomenal gift of service and grace."[7]

God is still moving mountains and using people of faith to do it. All the faith heroes of old and the faith warriors of today are united in one goal—trusting God to fulfill his promises:

> *"Yet all these, though they were commended for their faith, did not receive what was promised, since God had provided something better so that they would not, apart from us, be made perfect."*

HEBREWS 11:39-40

The preacher in Hebrews calls us to see the willingness of ordinary people to take extraordinary steps in faith for him. What seemingly impossible call has the Lord placed on your life?

---

[7]Ibid, 111.

Day 34

RUN THE RACE | Read Hebrews 12:1-3

While we may not accomplish individual success, our brokenness and humiliation in the service of God's Kingdom may further his divine plan in some way. This truth has been central to redemption history through the ages. God uses the folly of self-sacrifice to redeem and transform the world. It is the way of Jesus—the way of the cross.

Paul writes in 1 Corinthians 1:18: *"For the message about the cross is foolishness to those who are perishing, but to us who are being saved it is the power of God."* We may never know who will be inspired by our stand for what is right, but we should recognize that we are always being watched by those around us. We should never underestimate the power of a leader who is upright and walks with integrity to inspire others to the same.

In Christian terms, this is called our "witness." Are we willing to witness to truth, to patriotism, to good business practices, to great kindness? Most importantly, are we willing to witness to Jesus Christ?

The good news is, there is a *"great cloud of witnesses"* who serve as an eternal support system for us (Hebrews 12:1). These saints who have gone before show us the way of faith by their example and also, by their faith, stand with Jesus on the other side of the finish line cheering us on. Actually, the preacher paints the picture even more dramatically. They are the "cloud" witnesses. In the arenas of the ancient world, the highest seats in the arena were called the "seats in the clouds." The faithful believers and martyrs of old are literally in the grandstands of heaven cheering us on as those who have already run the race we are running and have already fought the good fight we are fighting.

These living witnesses are supporting and encouraging us to hold fast, hang tough, and keep going. By virtue of their faith, they have received the great salvation that is held out for us as we run *"the race that is set before us"* (Hebrews 12:1). Their witness for the faith has not gone unnoticed, and neither will yours!

The witness of any one martyr is costly in ways no other person can completely comprehend— financially, relationally, physically, and spiritually. And no one can dictate to another the manner of their sacrifice. The martyr is free to lay down his life as he or she believes God is asking, often unseen by believers around them. But that does not mean their witness goes unnoticed. The witness is often noted by those in opposition who may even be responsible for the trouble. But especially, the witness of the faithful sufferer never goes unnoticed by God. Whatever the worldly outcome, the Lord knows the attitudes of our heart and sees all. He will reward those who earnestly seek him.

Vindication for suffering in this life is a fleeting thing; even if it comes, it is ultimately temporary, unsatisfying, and inadequate. "*Vindication is mine; I will repay, says the Lord*" (Romans 12:19). There is comfort in that. But the greater reward is not found in either temporal or eternal vindication, but in the joy that is set before us. We are called to look to "*Jesus, the pioneer and perfecter of our faith, who for the sake of the joy that was set before him endured the cross, disregarding its shame, and has taken his seat at the right hand of the throne of God*" (Hebrews 12:2, NRSV).

Faith has eyes to see that the end is not the end. There is more to the story than what has currently been written, for we will have eternal joy shared with Jesus Christ in the throne room of heaven. He came down to the depths of earth to suffer greatly with us in order that he might capture us in his train and lead us straight to the heights of heaven. Such faith in the joy ahead enables victims of injustice to move on in life with peace and grace, to pray for the enemies who persecute them, and even at times to remain in relationship with them while showing them the grace, truth, goodness, and love of God. This unusual behavior is the unique mark of the Christian life—it is the mark of a disciple who has picked up his or her cross and followed Jesus, the mark of the martyr for faith. This truly is how the world is changed and redeemed for God.

Our world desperately needs men and women who will answer the call to be witnesses for Jesus Christ. Perhaps the Lord is calling you. God uses ordinary people to do extraordinary things. The key is not in your strength or power, but in your faith in Jesus' strength. God's power is made perfect in your weakness. Your job is to simply be faithful and stand firm, even if no one else is standing with you. That can feel quite foolish, but it is the right thing to do. And God will honor your faith. The message of the Cross of Jesus lies at the heart of God's plan of salvation for the world. The true Christian picks up his cross and follows Jesus in the foolish call of God.

How do we not lose heart in this race? In the wearying battle against sin and evil? The preacher of Hebrews tells us: by keeping our eyes firmly fixed on Jesus, our faith's author and perfecter. We need to stay close on his heels in the race. Take your eyes off Jesus and you will quickly be overwhelmed by the adversities and challenges of running without leadership, empathy, or direction. The preacher exhorts us to stay focused on the Lord: *"Consider him who endured such hostility against himself from sinners, so that you may not grow weary or lose heart."* (Hebrews 12:3).

In the same way that bikers and runners draft off the leader, Jesus takes the headwinds and gives us the help and the advantage. He sets the pace and shows us the route of the race—all the way to the finish line.

Reflection:

How do your life and actions bear witness to the works of Jesus Christ and the Living God?

Day 35

I was recently approached by a parishioner who requested:
"Would you please ask God why everything seems so hard for the faithful
and so easy for everyone else?"

What a great question! It resonates with the challenge of believing in
God and being faithful to him, the Church, and the Christian life when
the godless around us seem to prosper. Christians do not have it easy in
this world. In fact, at times it seems that the deck is stacked against us.
The preacher reminds us that it could be worse. Suffering is part of
life for the child of God. He calls us to recognize the opportunities for
growth and maturity in holiness afforded to us by suffering so we can
become the stronger, more mature people God is calling us to be.

To the preacher's first point, things could be worse in the *"struggle against
sin"* (Hebrews 12:4). Here he is speaking broadly of the general struggle
we all have against evil in all its forms, internal and external. The point
is, if we are still in the struggle, then we are still in the faith.

On one hand, the struggle with sin means our personal struggle with
our own sin. In this struggle, God is working to help us mature and
become holy. This is encouraging to me; it gives me hope in my struggles
against pride, procrastination, self-centeredness, and everything else. As
a committed Christian, I have struggled against my own sinful nature for
more than 25 years. As the Rev. Dr. Steve Brown often says, "I am better
than I was, but God is not through with me yet."

I am encouraged to know that there is meaning and significance behind
every hardship and suffering. And I am encouraged to know that
God is healing me of the self-inflicted wounds caused by my own sin-
centeredness through redemptive suffering.

Yet the struggle against sin is not just personal; it is also one of contending for the faith in an unbelieving and rebellious world. Let's face it: we live in a culture that avoids honest, truthful assessments and often refuses to confront glaring problems of character and morality. The parishioner's question above conveys a feeling of weariness with the ongoing struggle. "God, why is it so hard for the faithful?"

When we are experiencing trials, it is easy to fall into one of two dangers. The first is to take the struggle too lightly and not give it the weight and seriousness it is due.

The preacher encourages us not to ignore our suffering, but to see it as the Lord's loving discipline. When we are suffering, we should stand up and take notice. We should give the Lord our attention so that we might learn the lessons. Suffering is like parental discipline. It is not something we enjoy or desire. However, it shows us several things. It shows us that God cares about us as a parent does and wants us to be better. His discipline is intended to make us whole and righteous in spirit.

I have seen young children in public misbehaving, displaying bad character, and expressing themselves inappropriately. Since I am not their parent, I do not have the responsibility to discipline them. They are not my children. However, if I see one of my children needing correction or discipline, I engage. Why? Because I love them, and I am concerned about their character and maturity. They are my responsibility. The Lord's relationship is the same toward us. He loves us as a father does his beloved children.

There are two types of discipline that parents offer their children. One type is aimed at correcting sinful or bad actions, habits, and attitudes. This type of discipline is usually associated with very specific sins or behavior. For example, if the child makes a mess, they have to clean it up. Or worse, if they willfully rebel in disrespect, they will have a consequence. The "time out" or "restriction" of some privilege is a way to help the child feel some pain so as to discourage them from repeating the bad behavior. In the same way, the Lord will allow us to suffer consequences for our sin to help us change.

Romans 1 argues that because humans did not think it worthwhile to honor God or give him thanks, God handed them over to their own depraved thoughts, desires, and actions as a consequence. God eternally forgives his children of their sins through the blood of Jesus Christ. However, he still allows us to experience worldly consequences as a way of encouraging us toward repentance and faithfulness.

Another form of parental discipline comes in the teaching of strength, maturity, and growth. Many children do not like to do chores, go to school, or do homework. When I would ask my son what his favorite class at school was, he would always say, "recess!" It is important to understand the difference between the two types of discipline. Even children get confused. When they are young, they may think of homework as a punishment for something they did wrong, when in fact they have done everything well.

We once took our children's phones away from them at night. My daughter asked, "Why are you doing this? I am good kid! I make good choices!" And we agreed! We were not concerned about her choices or her behavior on the phone. We simply wanted her to rest from electronics and learn discipline.

Our Heavenly Father's concern in all of our trials is for our holiness. Whether they are trials that are specifically associated with our sin and rebellion, or whether they are to simply make us stronger and more perfect people:

> *Now, discipline always seems painful rather than pleasant at the time, but later it yields the peaceful fruit of righteousness to those who have been trained by it. Therefore lift your drooping hands and strengthen your weak knees, and make straight paths for your feet, so that what is lame may not be put out of joint, but rather be healed.*

HEBREWS 12:11, NRSV

If the first danger is to take suffering too lightly and not see it as the Lord's loving discipline, the second is to fall into discouragement and despair.

There are trials that we will go through in life that are not associated with a particular sin in our lives, but rather are simply to make us stronger, more mature, and holy people. Once we have examined our hearts and not found sin that God is rooting out with a particular discipline, we should rest in the peace of knowing he is working to mature us, to make us more like Jesus. But that doesn't mean these trials are easy.

I think of a wonderful Christian woman who had a wound that wouldn't heal—for 26 years! She had over 40 surgeries and procedures to try to mend the opening in her skin, but to no avail. She struggled to know what sin the Lord was trying to root from her. She came close to despair, yet she kept trusting there was a reason. Finally, she just accepted the trial as from the Lord's loving hand. She continued to pray for healing. At long last, the wound closed completely and has never reopened. And her testimony of faith over the long haul is an inspiration.

When the trials get too hard, it is tempting to become so discouraged that we throw in the towel and give up—to despair. But in light of the Cross, all suffering is redemptive for the faithful. When things get hard, the key is to allow the pain and trial to accomplish its desired effect in our life while holding on to the hand of Jesus for our strength.

Reflection:

You are a work in progress. The Lord loves you; he cares about you.
He uses suffering and trial to strengthen and heal us. As you look back
on moments of great suffering in your life, where have you seen the
experiences make you into a stronger, more holy person? Our attitude
and reaction to the discipline of the Lord can lead us away from God or
closer to him. Have you see examples where suffering has made you pull
away from the Lord?

Week 6

But you have come to Mount Zion and to the city of the living God, the heavenly Jerusalem, and to innumerable angels in festal gathering, and to the assembly of the firstborn who are enrolled in heaven, and to God, the judge of all, and to the spirits of the righteous made perfect, and to Jesus, the mediator of a new covenant, and to the sprinkled blood that speaks a better word than the blood of Abel.

HEBREWS 12:22-24

Day 36

DON'T BE LIKE ESAU | Read Hebrews 12:14-17

Every day, we have a choice as to how we will live. We can take the long view and see the blessing of living for the eternal kingdom or we can live shortsightedly and miss the "*grace of God* (Hebrews 12:15).

The simultaneous pursuits of both *holiness of life* and *peace with others* is the double challenge of living for Christ in an unholy world. If the preacher had given us just one challenge or the other, it would be easier. Peace with others is simple if we compromise and capitulate. But the call to holiness won't let us do that—Christians are called to be "set apart" from the world and its values.

Holiness gives us definition and boundaries for our relationships, our attitudes, our behaviors, and even our physical appearance. It will determine what we do with our time, talents, and treasures. It will give us an identity in God, telling us who we are and who we are not. Holiness sets us apart. Our purity of life will convict and condemn others who are not living such lives. Friendships, partnerships, and marriages will be strained if that purity is not shared. Those pressures can cause resentment towards God and towards others.

We are challenged to pursue holiness, which binds us to God. At the same time, we are challenged to pursue peace with everyone, which endears us to sinners. The great temptation is to allow the tension caused by the twin charges to move us to bitterness. We could grow bitter and resentful toward God for asking us to maintain this tension in the face of our pressures, trials, temptations, and persecutions. Bitterness is a root that will gradually bear a dangerous fruit. Bitterness sabotages our holiness, and without holiness, we will not see the Lord.

Bitterness can also lead toward unhelpful interactions with others. In our pursuit of holiness, self-righteous attitudes and pride can cause us to dissociate with others out of arrogance and anger. The sins of a poor disposition (pride, envy, arrogance, bitterness) are often the sins of the righteous. Here, we need to seek God's grace to help us. It is possible to fail to obtain the grace of God by falling into the ditch of self-righteousness.

Don't Be Like Esau!

An illustration from the time of the patriarchs is instructive. Esau was a son of Isaac and, by primogenitor, the favored son and heir of the Abrahamic line. However, Esau's downfall came during an encounter with his younger brother, Jacob. Knowing Esau was motivated by his stomach more than his brain, Jacob made a hungry Esau an offer he could not refuse: a bowl of delicious, warm soup in exchange for his birthright.

While in this biblical example it is very easy to see the foolishness of Esau in the exchange, the preacher is concerned that all of us are too often tempted to make the same exchange. When we choose to live a worldly life as opposed to a holy life, are we not choosing soup over our birthright? When we make the agenda of this world more important than the kingdom's agenda, have we not exchanged the comfort of the immediate for our eternal inheritance?

In the 2016 Rio Summer Olympics, Ryan Lochte, twelve-time Olympic medalist, apparently reveled in a night out on the town with his friends and then misrepresented it. "I over-exaggerated that story and if I had never done that we wouldn't be in this mess," he said in an interview aired on NBC. "None of this would have happened." Lochte, 32, blamed his "immature behavior."[1] Sadly, the consequences of Lochte's immature behavior were quite costly to him personally. In the wake of the bad press he received, four major sponsors withdrew their sponsorship, costing Lochte an estimated one million dollars.

Was the night of immature fun worth a million dollars? Was the bowl of

[1]http://edition.cnn.com/2016/08/20/sport/us-olympics-swimmers-reported-robbery-future/

soup worth the exchange of Esau's inheritance? The exchanges that we make on a daily basis are no less troubling. When we choose to follow the way of the world over Christ (because it will satisfy our temporal and fleshly appetites), we endanger our eternal inheritance. When we choose to disconnect from God and falter in the face of struggle and trial because holiness is too hard, we become like Esau.

Things didn't go so well for Esau. He missed out on much blessing because he looked at life through a godless lens. We live in a secular society that sees everything through a godless lens. In the worldly view, God is irrelevant and unimportant to daily life, thought, and behavior. But not to you! As a follower of Jesus, turn your eyes toward the Kingdom of God. Draw near to the Living God and allow him to bless you and give you an eternal inheritance.

Reflection:

How have you reconciled the call to remain holy with the call to make peace with others? Has it affected the company you keep?

Day 37

We live in an amazing phase of redemptive history. Prior to the coming of Jesus Christ, God was unapproachable and inaccessible to humanity. As human beings, we were profoundly disconnected from God. Since the beginning of human history, we have been barred from intimate fellowship with God because of sin. But that is *not* the way things are supposed to be. We were created for intimacy and fellowship with the divine creator of the universe. Our very nature is made in the image and likeness of God. God desires to be in communion with his people. Through that communion alone, we become a people that manifest a holy perfection and maturity.

In the Garden of Eden, the first man enjoyed an abiding friendship with God as he walked with him in the cool of the day. Joy, conversation, and relationship with God—these are experiences for which we are made.

The old hymn *In the Garden* captures the joy of divine fellowship in song:

> *And He walks with me, and He talks with me,*
> *And He tells me I am His own;*
> *And the joy we share as we tarry there,*
> *None other has ever known.*[2]

Oh, the joy of being able to experience the sweet fellowship of walking and talking with God! As people mired in the sluggish sea of a fallen world, we can be so disconnected from that kind of intimacy with God. We are weighed down by the mess around us. We no longer walk with God. We no longer talk with him. We forget that we are made for the purer waters of life and abundance and joy.

Sadly, not only do we *not miss* what we once had, we don't even realize that we *should* miss it! Distance and estrangement from God has become

[2]Charles A. Miles, In the Garden 1913

our "new normal"—so much so that movement toward the divine seems foreign, uncertain, and even unnatural to us. For many people in our world, even if they believe God is there, they view him as aloof and distant. Even for many religious people, God is to be feared and revered from a distance.

Indeed, that was the nature of humanity's relationship with God following the fall.

Think back to the garden and the incredible privilege our first parents enjoyed of intimacy with the Creator. God sang to them the divine melody, and it rang in their hearts. And yet, following the schemes of the evil angel Satan, they forsook the command of God and forfeited their life of fellowship with the God. With their disobedience came the knowledge of both good and evil, leading to broken fellowship with the Creator and a fierce distance. Our first parents were driven out of the grand garden of God:

> "So the Lord God banished him from the Garden of Eden to work the ground from which he had been taken. After he drove the man out, he placed on the east side of the Garden of Eden cherubim and a flaming sword flashing back and forth to guard the way to the tree of life"

GENESIS 3:23-24

Access to divine fellowship and the blessings of eternal life in God were seeming lost forever to humanity. A flaming, slashing sword and angelic cherubim prevented access to the inner sanctum of divine fellowship and the paradise of God for most of human history. Broken fellowship leads to corruption. Humanity disintegrated morally, spiritually, and relationally. The first murder in the Bible is perpetrated by none other than Adam and Eve's firstborn son, Cain. He was warned that "*sin is lurking at the door; its desire is for you, but you must master it*" (Genesis 4:7b). Yet, Cain chose to succumb. Sin is lurking. Such a simple three-letter word: SIN. But it represents everything bad about humanity apart from God. Sin is both action and condition. Sin is nature and practice. We sin. We are sinners.

Indeed, to enter into the holy chambers of the Living God as guilty sinners is a dreadful thing. Ask those who approached Mount Sinai "...*a blazing fire, and darkness, and gloom, and a tempest, and the sound of a trumpet, and a voice whose words made the hearers beg that not another word be spoken to them*" (Hebrews 12:18-19).

Even Moses said, "*I tremble with fear!*"

Many prophets of old had done so as well. Those taken into that inner sanctum such as Moses, Elijah, Jeremiah, and Isaiah experienced the dreadful presence. Isaiah's response to the throne room of God was an experience of personal disintegration and fear. As he beheld the divine majesty, a rush of clarity regarding his own impurity flooded his consciousness:

> *In the year that King Uzziah died I saw the Lord sitting upon a throne, high and lifted up; and the train of his robe filled the temple. Above him stood the seraphim. Each had six wings: with two he covered his face, and with two he covered his feet, and with two he flew. And one called to another and said:*
>
> *Holy, holy, holy is the Lord of hosts;*
> *the whole earth is full of his glory!'*
> *And the foundations of the thresholds shook at the voice of him who called, and the house was filled with smoke. And I said:'Woe is me! For I am lost; for I am a man of unclean lips, and I dwell in the midst of a people of unclean lips; for my eyes have seen the King, the Lord of hosts!'*

ISAIAH 6:1-5

Just as with Isaiah, guilt and shame are powerful forces in our lives. They can drive us into a spiritual and relational hiding place estranged from God and others. When confronted with holiness, shame keeps us secreted behind seemingly invulnerable facades and niceties. We cover ourselves and hide out of fear of being truly seen and truly known.

Yet, just as the Lord made a way for Isaiah to stand before him, so he has done for us. Through Jesus, the Son of God, and our Great High Priest, we now have access to stand boldly before the throne of grace without fear of judgement or condemnation.

The Lord invites us to an *approachable* and *accessible* mountain, Mount Zion, the New Jerusalem. This mountain is described as a tremendous assembly of saints and angelic hosts gathered in joyous worship. When we gather in worship here on earth, we are invited by the Word, Jesus Christ, to come up and take part, to revel with "*the assembly of the first born whose names are written in heaven*" and to praise and worship the Living God along with the "*spirits of the righteous made perfect*" (Hebrews 12:23).

The sin, guilt, shame, and death of the old order are represented as the word of the blood of Abel. That word cries out for our judgment and to estrange us from God. But because of the New Covenant in Jesus, a better blood speaks a better word. Jesus' blood invites us into the Holy of Holies and provides us full access to, in the words of the hymn *The Church's One Foundation*, "mystic sweet communion with those whose rest is won":

> O happy ones and holy!
> Lord, give us grace that we
> Like them, the meek and lowly,
> On high may dwell with Thee[3]

With the advent of Jesus, human beings are now offered direct access to the Living God in a new and living way of interpersonal relationship with him. The book of Hebrews not only teaches us the way to move into connected intimate fellowship with God, it implores us to realize that our very life depends on it. As the preacher will say "*our God is a consuming fire*" (Hebrews 12:29).

[3]Samuel John Stone, The Church's One Foundation

Reflection:

Use your imagination to experience what it might have been like to walk with God in the Garden, in the cool of the evening. Can you imagine yourself beside God, walking and talking freely? Do so now. Your sin and shame have been wiped away by Jesus. You are shining and pure in God's eyes. Enjoy speaking, laughing, and sharing with him as his beloved child right now!

_____

_____

_____

_____

Day 38

The Didache, meaning teaching, represents one of the earliest catechisms of the Church. The full title is Teaching of the Twelve Apostles. This account gives clear insight into the Early Church practice of keeping the uninitiated from the table. Written before 300 A.D., it provides a compilation of basic instructions from the Scriptures: "And let none eat or drink of your Eucharist but such as have been baptized into the name of the Lord, for of a truth the Lord has said concerning this, give not that which is holy unto dogs." (The Didache, 95 A.D.)

Jarringly, the reference to *dogs* in the sentence is taken from the words of Jesus. In the Sermon on the Mount, Jesus taught, *"Do not give what is holy to dogs; and do not throw your pearls before swine, or they will trample them under foot and turn and maul you."* (Matthew 7:6). Lay Christians and theologians from the first three centuries through the time of the Reformation (and to our day in the Anglican communion) associated this verse with the Eucharist. Later, in Matthew's Gospel, Jesus again uses the term *dogs* in reference to non-Jews as compared to the Israelite *children*. We read of an interaction with a Canaanite woman asking for an exorcism for her possessed daughter.

> *But she came and knelt before him, saying, "Lord, help me." He answered, "It is not fair to take the children's food and throw it to the dogs." She said, "Yes, Lord, yet even the dogs eat the crumbs that fall from their masters' table." Then Jesus answered her, "Woman, great is your faith! Let it be done for you as you wish." And her daughter was healed instantly.*

MATTHEW 15:25-28

Moved by the humility and faith of the woman, Jesus commends her and welcomes her into the power of the Messianic kingdom. In 1548, Archbishop Thomas Cranmer captured the heart of this exchange and incorporated the faith of the Canaanite woman into *The Book of Common Prayer* in a collect known as the Prayer of Humble Access. This prayer may be said by the entire worshiping congregation following the Eucharistic prayer and right before taking communion:

> *We do not presume to come to this thy Table, O merciful Lord, trusting in our own righteousness, but in thy manifold and great mercies. We are not worthy so much as to gather up the crumbs under thy Table. But thou art the same Lord whose property is always to have mercy. Grant us, therefore, gracious Lord, so to eat the flesh of thy dear Son Jesus Christ, and to drink his blood, that we may evermore dwell in him, and he in us. Amen.*

BCP P. 337

Reflecting on the prayer, Katie Badie reflects that "Cranmer thus evokes the intimate living and personal relationship of the believer with Christ. The request of the Prayer of Humble Access is that Communion should be a moment when this relationship of faith is strengthened and nourished, producing the desired fruit for eternity (John 15:5)."

The Eucharist is holy. We are not worthy to partake of the presence of God, yet this is what we are being invited to do. We access the Lord through faith and humility. We access the Lord through abundant grace by his invitation. The Canaanite woman exemplifies this dynamic and the Lord commends it. A primary concern of the Book of Hebrews is to encourage such humble boldness in response to the mercy of God through the Cross of Christ. We are being invited to hear the promise of salvation, to make the confession of faith, and then *"approach the throne of grace with boldness"* (Hebrews 4:16). Such boldness is not without humility.

As the worshiper enters the presence of the assembly of the church, the King of Kings and the Lord of Lords is present. As he said, *"when two or more are gathered in my name, I am there in the midst of you"* (Matthew 18:20), and in another place he says, *"All authority in heaven and on earth has been given to me.... And remember, I am with you always, to the end of the age."* (Matthew 28:18, 20).

The king walks among the lampstands of his churches (Revelation 1:13). Indeed, Jesus is present with this people in the assembly.

This is why reverent gestures are appropriate as Christians enter their churches. A bow of the head or even the more expressive genuflection (bending one knee to Jesus' majesty) have been common practice since the early Church. King Jesus is present and we pay him respect as we enter the sanctuary, his holy ground (think of Moses removing his sandals in God's presence). We approach God's throne with a paradoxical bold humility at his most gracious invitation.

Word and Sacraments

And so the book of Hebrews is primarily about the work of the people of God in worshiping the Living God. The word for that "people work" is liturgy (Latin. *leit-* people + *ergon* work). The form of the divine liturgy is aimed at engaging the worshiper in active ministry to the one true God. At a basic level there are two main parts of the divine liturgy—the Ministry of the Word and the Ministry of the Sacrament.

These two things that we do in Christian liturgy as Anglicans are not unique to us: Orthodox, Catholics, Lutherans, Methodists, and many others recognize this pattern. It is the ancient pattern of Christian worship, practiced for millennia. It's worth reiterating a quote I shared earlier in the book. The Rev. Richard Hooker once observed that "if the Liturgies of all ancient Churches throughout the world be compared amongst themselves, it may be easily perceived they had all one original mold. (Ecclesiastical Polity, Book V Ch. 25). Indeed, we can discern this original mold in the book of Hebrews.

The first several chapters of the book correspond with the Ministry of the Word. The writer of Hebrews argues for the supremacy of the Son of God as the Word made flesh. This word is greater than the spoken word given by angels to Moses and the prophets. It is a word to which the worshiper must pay rapt attention as it is a word of great salvation. The word calls us to enter into the Sabbath rest that is held out for the people of God. Or work is to respond with open hearts. The Word, Jesus, speaks to us is the word (the Scriptures) and it is a piercing two-edged sword which will plunge deeply into the core of our being and convict our hearts.

The second third of Hebrews, chapters four through twelve, are about the Ministry of the Sacrament mediated to us by our Great High Priest. We are called to draw in to the throne room of grace. There the Great High Priest will minister to us by his sacrifice of himself, offered once for all, but also through his perpetual intercession for us at the throne of God. By faith, we believe the promises of Jesus' word and we approach the Holy Mountain of God with confidence, in humility.

The final chapter of the sermon to the Hebrews is about living by faith in the world as a sacrifice: by the way we serve others in hospitality and care, by the way we live in holiness within the community of the faithful, and by the way we bear the reproach of Christ outside the community.

Reflection:

Which is more natural for you—to approach the throne of God with humility or with boldness? How can you work on experiencing both attitudes as you come into the Holy of Holies with Jesus in worship?

Day 39

For 40 years, the nation of Israel wandered in the Sinai wilderness between Egypt and the Promised Land. They had very specific instructions as to how to set up camp, live in community, and associate with those outside the community. Their camp took a specific shape when it was set up correctly—a cruciform.

> What a sight to stand upon a vista and gaze down upon the tents of Israel. "Balaam said of the Israelite camps: 'How beautiful are your tents, O Jacob, your dwelling places, O Israel!'"
>
> **NUMBERS 24:5**

Throughout the book of Hebrews, the preacher has primarily been focused on our relationship with God during worship, using the metaphor and imagery of the Old Covenant people of God who made camp in the desert on the way to the Promised Land. The tent of meeting, with its inner sanctuary, priesthood, and sacrifices is a shadow and symbol of the Great Salvation offered through the Great High Priest. By his perfect sacrifice of himself once offered, we have access to the heavenly sanctuary by faith.

A restored relationship with God through Christ Jesus will manifest in restored relationships with others. Just as the shape of the Israelites' camp took a cruciform shape with worship of the Living God at the center of community life, so too will the shape of our relationships be patterned after the Cross when the living sanctuary is central.

As we approach the end of the book, the final thoughts of the preacher turn toward answering the question, "How shall we then live?" In light of our faith-filled worship of the Living God, what should our lives look like? What is the practical application of our holy relationship with the Living God? This question has two primary aspects:

How should we live relationally *inside the camp* as God's holy chosen people?

How should we live *outside the camp* as those who, in unity with Christ, bear reproach?

In both cases, we are to see our lives as united with Jesus, who lived in righteousness and holiness relationally: showing hospitality, caring for the marginalized and mistreated of God's people, maintaining holiness in marriage and chastity in life, and pursuing contentment rather than the love of money.

phil-adelphia – love for the brotherhood

Continuous mutual love (brotherly love, in Greek *phil-adelphia*) anchors the heart in the life of Christ. He sacrificed for us as his brothers and sisters; therefore, our continual sacrifice is to offer our lives and love to one another as the family of God (Hebrews 2:11-12). Our mutual love is an aspect of the *"unshakable kingdom"* which we are inheriting. As Paul reminds us in 1 Corinthians 13, love is one of the three things that will *"remain"* after all else comes to an end. At the last hour, the only things that will matter are our abiding relationship with God and our relationships with one another. All else is secondary. Our love for one another is eternal; it continues forever. It never ends.

If we are urged to show love to the believers in our midst, we are also charged to remember the Christian brothers and sisters who are far from our immediate presence, trapped in prison. In the days of the Early Church, one could become imprisoned for simply being a believer in Jesus Christ, just as we see in parts of the Middle East today. Christians were persecuted and mistreated for their insistence on singular personal allegiance to Jesus Christ.

The preacher exhorts that even though our Christian brothers and sisters are away from us or imprisoned, they are still connected to us in the body of Christ and the household of God. We must always remember to pray for them and visit them when possible. In 2013, the US Bureau of Justice Statistics reported that there are 2,220,300 people in state and federal prisons and county jails. While it's difficult to be exact, researchers estimate that between 50-60% of this population identifies themselves as Christian (either Protestant or Catholic).

We forget that we were once prisoners—to Satan, sin, and death. In our imprisonment, Jesus came in solidarity with us, experiencing death for us in order to free us from its chains:

> *Since, therefore, the children share flesh and blood, he himself likewise shared the same things, so that through death he might destroy the one who has the power of death, that is, the devil, and free those who all their lives were held in slavery by the fear of death.*

HEBREWS 2:14-15

Our stand in solidarity with believers who are imprisoned or mistreated reflects our unity in Jesus Christ. He came to us when we were in prison. Jesus is the great liberator. When our brothers and sisters in Jesus are behind bars, we are with them. When they are mistreated, so are we. We are one.

philo-xenia – kove for the stranger

As followers of Jesus, we are called not just to love our own, but also to show hospitality and care to the stranger. Though this command can produce a tension between personal holiness and a life of reaching out, they are not mutually exclusive; in fact, they are two sides of the same coin. To "be holy" means to "be set apart," but does that mean that hospitality to outsiders goes out the window? Are the boundaries to be set so strongly that the Christian should not even associate with strangers or non-believers? Xenophobia is the fear of the stranger. Often a tight group can be overly concerned about the influence of an outside group or person. Their cultures and customs are often strange and perceived as a threat to identity and purity. (The Amish remain largely cloistered from outsiders in an attempt to preserve personal and community purity.)

But God has not called us to live removed from the world! On the contrary, once we are secure in our relationship to God, our identity in him, and our manner of life as believers, we can freely relate to the stranger (*xenoi*) with love. The call is to love and welcome the stranger with a posture of hospitality and grace. Inside the camp, the people of God are called to be holy in their relationships with one another. However, it is a loving holiness that extends beyond itself.

When we are focused exclusively on our existing relationships, we easily forget to look around and show care to the new person or the unknown visitor in our midst. It is heartbreaking to hear from new members how they visited other churches, and no one said a word to them—they walked in and walked out without so much as a greeting or any attempt of welcome. May it not be so in our churches!

The call to show hospitality runs deep in the story of Israel. Abraham is blessed by welcoming three strangers who turned out to be messengers of good news, who spoke prophetically as angels of the Lord. The strangers and visitors in our midst may have been sent by God to bring some missing spiritual gift to us, or to meet a need where it was lacking. At one time, Jesus came as a stranger to this world, and to those "*who received him, who believed in his name, he gave the right to become children of God*" (John 1:12). Let us welcome the stranger while never forgetting that our first priority is to care for our brothers and sisters in Christ.

Reflection:

How do we perceive the stranger in the midst of our assemblies? What does it feel like to be the lone outsider with a group of insiders? Do Christians have a unique role to play with respect to immigrants and foreigners in our country? How can the church more effectively care for our brothers and sisters in Christ behind bars?

Day 40

Just like the faithful people of old, followers of Jesus must exhibit holiness of life inside the camp—even more so, for the community of the faithful in Jesus is nothing less than the living temple of the Holy, Holy, Holy God. We are his dwelling place and inner sanctum! We must be holy.

Marriage

The call to holiness is a call to sexual purity. Upholding the sanctity of marriage is a hallmark of Jesus' teaching. He was very strict on divorce, encouraged lifelong monogamous marriage between a man and a woman, and encouraged abstinence from sexual immorality in all its forms. Sexual relations are good and holy within the godly confines of marriage, but a sexual relationship outside of marriage shows disrespect for the institution itself. The preacher underscores the Lord's teaching with the positive vision of a pure marriage bed.

What is the significance of the marriage bed and why is it important to keep it undefiled? For most of the sermon, the preacher has been explaining the invitation and call to *"draw near"* to the Living God. Out of all our human relationships, marriage alone represents a sacramental vision of the holy relationship between God and his people. The marriage bed is the *"most holy place"* for human intimacy. Just as we do not defile the body and blood of Jesus that ushers us into the divine chamber, so too should we not defile the marriage bed. As Paul taught elsewhere, marriage between a husband and wife mysteriously reveals Christ's relationship to the Church and the loving sacrifice that Jesus makes for us.

I would say that most of the couples that come to me for marriage counseling are co-habiting and engaging in fornication, which means having sexual relations outside of marriage. The pressure is on from our culture. It was not too long ago that a marriage bed shown on TV would be scandalous. Now movies and TV regularly portray couples in bed merely as a romantic consummation of a good fling.

The other challenge to our pure marriage bed is not simply the content of TV, electronic devices, and internet use, as egregious as that is, but simply the presence of too much electronic media. We often find ourselves scrolling through our phones and tablets instead of reconnecting with our spouses or choosing a football game or favorite show instead of a date night.

Between the cultural pressures of pre-marital sex and the addicting nature of screen time, it's difficult to maintain the marriage bed as a sacred space, but we are called to do so as Christians.

Besides pornography and screen addiction, there's another threat to our relationship with Christ and others inside the camp: the love of money.

phil-argyria love of money

Not all loves are good. While love of the brotherhood (**philadelphia**) and love of the stranger (**philoxenia**) are encouraged, love of money (**philagyria**) is clearly discouraged. Paul calls "*love of money*" the root of all evil:

> "*For the love of money is a root of all kinds of evil, and in their eagerness to be rich some have wandered away from the faith and pierced themselves with many pains*"

1 TIMOTHY 6:10

Jesus spoke more about money and its dangers than any other topic. Of the 39 parables Jesus tells, eleven are about financial matters. The preacher of Hebrews tells us to "*keep our lives free from the love of money.*" The book of Hebrews is primarily about intimacy and relationship with the Living God and, if we love money, we will lose our love for and intimacy with the Lord. Jesus taught that these two loves are mutually exclusive:

"No one can serve two masters; for a slave will either hate the one and love the other, or be devoted to the one and despise the other. You cannot serve God and wealth"

The key to staying free from love of money is to learn to be content with what we have been given. Everything we have is a gift from the hand of the Lord. He is our provider and ever present help.

Contentment is directly related to valuing God's covenant promises to us above material comforts.

Godly Leaders and False Leaders

There are two types of leadership manifest within the household of God—true and false. True and godly teaching stays true to Jesus' message and that of the apostles. Faithful teaching exalts Jesus as the supreme kingly Lord of the Church and the Great High Priest. It calls people to holiness of life; it is exemplified by godly character.

God's word and its application to our lives is eternal—it never becomes irrelevant or out of date.

False teaching often centers on a legalistic system of rules and regulations (such as food laws). The external legalism is a mask for internal distance from personal holiness that comes from true intimacy with the Lord. Such intimacy is only possible through grace. Legalism misses the grace offered to us.

I have had the occasion to personally interact with two controversial teachers well known for their public denials of basic doctrines of the faith such as the bodily resurrection of Jesus.

In discussions with both of them, I sought to get to the assumptions that were driving their beliefs. Both held to an impersonal God who doesn't perform miracles and is not involved directly in the lives of people; instead, this "god" allows people to do basically whatever they want, particularly in the area of sexual morality.

Both of these men had people in their lives whom they cared about, spouses and children, who either suffered from exposure to or had lifestyles that did not fit with the Christian moral life. Rather than recognizing the tension, they adjusted their theological assumptions to allow for a teaching that excused or embraced the behavior of their loved one.

Behavior shapes beliefs. Immoral behavior corrupts good doctrine. False and strange teachings are often created as a way of excusing or explaining away the challenges to faithfulness. These alterations of belief represent either a capitulation to cultural pressures, a fear of man, and/ or a desire to gratify the flesh.

The doctrines of grace, in contrast, enable the believer to be absolutely sober-minded about sin and falsehood while, at the same time, maintaining humility and room for every individual's personal growth in relationship with God.

Reflection:

How can you guard your life against the constant barrage of false teaching, lustful media, and money-obsessed culture? Which of these things challenge you the most, and what can you do to remind yourself to pursue purity in all its forms?

Day 41

OUTSIDE THE CAMP | Read Hebrews 13:11-19

Just as Jesus ventured outside the camp of God's Kingdom to show us the way to salvation, so must we venture outside the camp of our communities to spread the word of the Lord.

Using the imagery of animal sacrifices being burned outside the camp, the writer urges us to see Jesus as the sacrifice who bore reproach, one crucified outside the camp. As we are called to live like Jesus, we must join him in reproach outside the camp. We are cozy and comfortable in our camp! And, while building bonds within the Christian community is important, we must have the courage to mobilize our worship community to do good for others, to bear witness to the Lord's great mercy outside the camp. It's all well and good to worship the Lord in peace, but true faith shines even brighter in the face of derision.

Outside the camp, people of God will encounter all kinds of opposition. I met a woman in my travels who rededicated her life to the Lord through baptism. It was a beautiful ceremony and she was ecstatic about her decision. I could see the light of God's mercy at work in her. In her excitement, she posted photos of the baptism on her social media because she longed to share the incredible peace she had found with the people she knew and loved. Much to her dismay, people she knew began to post mocking comments under the photos. They ridiculed her for her recommitment and her family scorned her, saying all kinds of terrible things. The woman was hurt. I had to remind her that Christians are often met by this type of mocking reproach. She stood strong in her faith, but I know it was not easy for her.

Often the rejection of earthly ways by true believers of Christ convicts non-believers of their sin. When a non-believer sees someone rejoice in their salvation through Jesus, they are reminded of their spiritual shortcomings. Because they long for that grace but rebel against it, they often lash out in anger or fear, much like a wounded animal. Rebellious hearts either submit to the mercy of the Lord or they scorn it. Those who scorn salvation will hate you for being devoted to God, and they might ostracize or disown you.

Not only will Christians face mockery for their faith, but they will also be targeted by false teachers. The world is chock full of "snake oil" and "fool's gold" salesmen who would like to convince you that their product is the real thing. It is not easy to be an advocate for truth, kindness, and God's love in a world of tricksters and frauds, but that is what we are called to do. Jesus underwent extreme scrutiny during his time on earth. He was ridiculed and reproached as he stood for the truth. And we are called to live as he did. 1 Peter 4:14-16 says, *"If you are insulted for the name of Christ, you are blessed, because the Spirit of glory and of God rests upon you. But let none of you suffer as a murderer or an evildoer or as a meddler. Yet is anyone suffers as a Christian let him not be ashamed, but left him glorify God in that name."*

Despite the reproach we may face and the dangers of a sinful world, there are people outside of the camp who need to hear the message of Jesus. There are sinners who long for salvation but who have not encountered one true believer. They are defensive and afraid because they have never been met with the kindness of God or they have met frauds and blasphemers disguised as Christians. In sweet and winsome contrast, we must serve as positive and true examples of the love of God.

The stakes are sometimes very high, but you are called to reveal yourself as a Christian—believers cannot hide in the shadows. It's like the gospel song often sung by children, "This Little Light of Mine," written in the 1920's by Henry Dixon Loes. I'm sure you know the song, but you may not know that it's based on Matthew 5:14-16: *"You are the light of the world. A city on a hill cannot be hidden. Nor do people light a lamp and put it under a basket, but on a stand, and it gives light to all in the house. In the same way, let your light shine before others, so that they may see your good works and give glory to your Father who is in heaven."* We cannot hide our light inside the camp, but rather, we must stand on the rooftops and proclaim the good news of Jesus.

When we sacrifice our egos and social standing in order to share the word of God, it pleases Him. Our call is not only to bear the same reproach as he did in this sinful and broken world, but also to share our possessions and do godly work in his name. Though the world knocks us down, we can stand tall and carry on knowing that we have eternal salvation through Jesus so long as we persevere!

Reflection:

Where do you find the strength to persevere in this sinful and fallen world?

Day 42

The book of Hebrews challenges Christians to remember the importance of intimacy with God, communion, and community. The preacher lays out a complex argument for the supremacy of Jesus, the significance of the New Covenant versus the Old, and the consequences of faithful versus sinful lives. His main concern is for the members of the congregation who have begun to slip away and falter—he calls for their swift return to the fold.

The preacher also calls for a system of encouragement between members, reviews how to be a faithful Christian, and explains proper worship to restore its meaning and significance. Mostly, though, he calls for greater attention to every detail of one's spiritual life, through intimacy with Jesus.

To worship the Lord is to bless and to be blessed. And so, the preacher to the Hebrews offers his audience a blessing before he signs off. He calls Jesus *"the great shepherd of the sheep,"* which is reminiscent of the first part of Psalm 23: *"The Lord is my shepherd; I shall not want. He makes me lie down in green pastures. He leads me beside still waters. He restores my soul. He leads me in paths of righteousness for his name's sake"* (Psalm 23:1-3).

Psalm 23 is the perfect benediction to the book of Hebrews because it echoes the preacher's rhetoric to stay close to God. Like sheep following a shepherd, the pastor reminds us that we must trust and obey the Lord. We know we can trust in his word because he kept his promises to Abraham and Moses—the Lord made a nation of Abraham and provided for the Israelites as they trekked to the Promised Land. God will always provide for his people, and through the New Covenant, Jesus can truly restore our hearts and souls by cleansing them of sin. He provides for us in our earthly lives and for our eternal lives. Once we open our hearts to Jesus' healing love, the law of the New Covenant is etched in our minds as a perpetual reminder to keep the righteous path. Through the salvation of Jesus, we can enjoy the green pastures and still waters of Sabbath rest.

Psalm 23 continues, *"Even though I walk through the valley of the shadow of death, I will fear no evil, for you are with me; your rod and your staff, they comfort me"* (Psalm 23:4). The world is a terrifying place, full of sin, shame, and death. But God is always with those who are intimate with him. Jesus walked among men to experience the toils of life so that he could empathize with us, and he is our eternal priest, forever there to comfort those who call on him. There's no reason to fear death when Jesus has taken off the shackles of mortality and given us eternal life with God.

Hebrews reminds us that the Lord is preparing a heavenly bounty for us. Psalm 23:5 says, *"You prepare a table before me in the presence of my enemies; you anoint my head with oil; my cup overflows."* This heavenly bounty has already begun. The New Covenant offers us a table of Holy Communion—a table prepared before us by God—every week in worship. God anointed his son as our eternal priest. His grace and mercy fills our cups until they overflow. And when we live in the abundance of his favor, our lives bear the fruit of the Spirit. The prayer of Psalm 23 concludes, *"Surely goodness and mercy shall follow me all the days of my life, and I shall dwell in the house of the Lord forever."* The driving point of Hebrews is that the reward of full assurance of faith in the Lord is eternal life in the heavenly throne room (Psalm 23:6). God's will is togetherness, and it is by his will that we have been granted access to the house of the Lord.

True intimacy with the Lord starts with a confession of faith in worship, and it is consummated with the ritual of communion. To be intimate is to know someone deeply; we grow in intimacy with God when we know him more fully. When we enjoy God through his beautiful creations, sing a hymn to him, offer a tithe to his Church, or do something kind for another person in remembrance of him, we honor him. When we enjoy the Lord, he enjoys us, and nothing satisfies God more than closeness with his children. Jesus has taken away all the obstacles to salvation, and nothing can stop you from getting close to God except your own lack of desire, capitulation to weakness, or simple rebellion.

Every day we make a choice to follow God. So every day is an opportunity to draw closer, to lean in, and to fall head over heels in holy love. But that also means that every day is an opportunity to lose faith and wander away from his holy light. Remember the exhortation of the preacher that we must pay much closer attention to what we have heard... *"lest we drift away"* (Hebrews 2:1).

Rather than drift away, let us resolve to pay close attention to the Great Salvation offered by our Great High Priest and *"...draw near with confidence to the throne of grace"* where, in intimacy with God through Jesus Christ, in the Holy of Holies, will find our Sabbath Rest.

Reflection:

Think over the past six weeks. What realizations have you come to about your faith? What new purposes have you set for yourself? What will stick with you from this course?

> *You prepare a table before me*
> *in the presence of my enemies;*
> *you anoint my head with oil;*
> *my cup overflows.*
> *Surely goodness and mercy shall follow me*
> *all the days of my life,*
> *and I shall dwell in the house of the Lord forever.*

PSALM 23:5-6

The
StudyGuide

Using this Study
Outline of Each Session

APPENDICES

Frequently Asked Questions
Small Group Covenant
Group Calendar
Prayer and Priase Report
Small Group Roster

SMALL GROUP LEADER HELPS

Hosting an Open House
Leading for the First Time
Leadership Training 101

Using this Study

HOW TO GET THE MOST OUT OF THIS STUDY

As with any individual or small-group study of God's word, you largely reap what you sow—or, as it is commonly put, you get out of it what you put into it. But additionally, there are guidelines that can help you get the most from the efforts you put in. I've outlined some suggestions here for you and your group to review before you get started.

1. Review the Table of Contents.

2. The section entitled "Small Group Leader Helps" lays out best practices for how to host and facilitate a healthy small group and avoid common mistakes. It's a great idea to review this material before having your first meeting.

3. This book is a tool for facilitation. Adapt it to the needs of your group. If a line of discussion leads to green pastures outside the scope of the book, enjoy the leading of the Good Shepherd. Feel free to ask, or allow other members to ask, insightful questions as the Holy Spirit leads.

4. There is a lot of material here. You do not have to ask every question in your group discussion. Feel free to skip questions as needed and linger over the ones where there is authentic conversation.

5. Enjoy the experience. Christian community should be characterized by joy and love. Encourage yourself and the group members to bear such fruit.

6. Pray before each session—ask God to minister to you, the facilitator, and every group member by name. Pray for the discussion, the fellowship, and the personal application.

7. Read the "Outline of Each Session" on the following pages so you understand the flow of the session and how the study works.

Outline of Each Session

KEY VERSE

Each session begins with a key verse. This verse is a key to understanding the entire week's theme. You may want to memorize these verses. By committing portions of God's Word to long-term memory, you will always have them to refer to even when you don't have a Bible with you.

PAY ATTENTION TO THE WORD

When the book of Hebrews quotes an Old Testament Scripture, it is often prefaced by "God says..." or the "Holy Spirit says..." The writer is reminding us that God is speaking to us in his Word. This is a good reminder that the Word of God is "living and active," speaking not just when it was written, but into our hearts and lives today. Our first task, then, is to pay attention and hear what God is saying to us in his Word.

The video segment will provide teaching on the passage and direction for the session, serving as a launching pad for your discussion. There will also be a section of Scripture for the group to read aloud. Questions will follow to help group members make observations and interpret the text. Use as many or as few of these questions as prove helpful.

STUDY NOTES

These pages provide a space to take notes as you watch the video or hear inspirational thoughts from the Lord or members of your group.

DRAW NEAR TO THE THRONE

As we hear God's Word together, we are called to respond by being drawn into communion with God and community with one another. The second section of every study will seek to call your hearts to greater intimacy and vulnerability with God and your brothers and sisters in Christ.
The questions in this section will invite you to apply what you are learning through fellowship, prayer, and corporate worship.

RUN THE RACE SET BEFORE YOU

The writer of Hebrews describes the life of a believer as a test of enduring faith. We are called to keep our eyes fixed on Jesus as we set out to be faithful to him. This section will explore the challenges of being faithful in a faithless world. Each session will seek to find ways to practically bear witness for Jesus Christ both within the community of believers and outside the Church, in the world.

DAILY DEVOTIONS

Studying the book of Hebrews is like mining a rich vein of gold. The deeper you dig, the more treasure you will discover. Set aside time to spend with the Lord each day. The devotions will give you a brief portion of Scripture to read and a short meditation to stimulate your personal interaction with God and his Word. Pray and ask the Lord to reveal himself to you. Use the space provided to journal what you are hearing from the Lord or to express your prayers and praises.

1

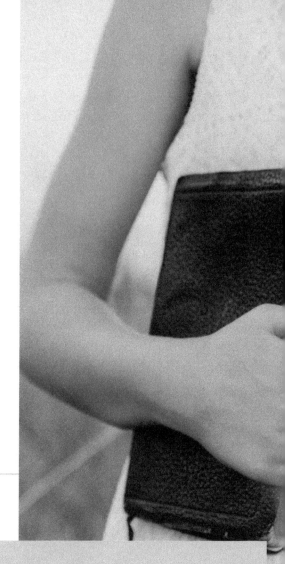

ATTENDING TO THE WORD OF THE LORD

KEY VERSE

Therefore, we must pay much closer attention to what we have heard, lest we drift away from it. For since the message declared by angels proved to be reliable, and every transgression or disobedience received a just retribution, how shall we escape if we neglect such a great salvation? — HEBREWS 2:1-3A

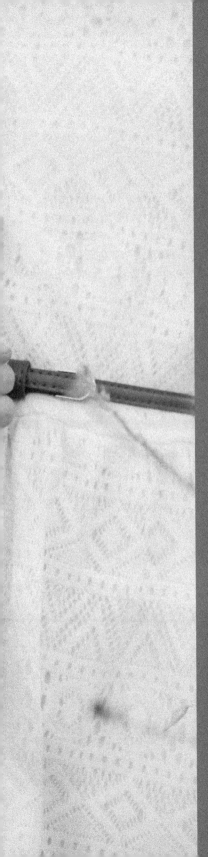

SESSION INTRODUCTION:

An angel is a divine messenger. In the Old Testament, angels were employed by God to deliver his messages to Moses and the prophets. In Jesus, the Word of God is made flesh. Just as the Son is superior to the angels, so the message delivered through the Son is superior. Jesus is the supreme messenger of God.

The message of the angels was true and to disobey their words brought judgement. How much more should the message of the Son demand our attention and response? The preacher calls the message of the Son "a great salvation" (2:3). We are saved from the power of death by the Son who tasted death for us that we might taste his glory with him. He partook of our flesh and blood that we might partake of his saving flesh and blood.

Every week when we come into a liturgical worship service, we hear the Word of God read and preached. It is important to recognize not only who is speaking to us, but what is being offered to us. You are being offered a share in the Great Salvation through Jesus Christ. Will your heart be in a state of hopeful confidence toward the Lord and his Word or stubbornly withdrawn? Reach out to him. How can the Savior help you today?

Opening Prayer

USE THIS PRAYER OR PRAY ONE OF YOUR
OWN. YOU MAY WANT TO SAY IT TOGETHER.

*Blessed Lord, who caused all holy Scriptures to be written for our
learning: Grant us so to hear them, read, mark, learn, and inwardly
digest them, that we may embrace and ever hold fast the blessed hope of everlasting life, which you have given us in our Savior
Jesus Christ; who lives and reigns with you and the Holy Spirit, one
God, for ever and
ever. Amen.*

—Book of Common Prayer (BCP) p. 236.

GETTING STARTED

1. Why can it be so difficult to pay attention during a church service?

2. Tell about a time when you really heard God speak to you in a
   church service.

WATCH THE VIDEO / SESSION 1
https://biblestudymedia.com/drawnear/

Pay Attention to the Word

When the book of Hebrews quotes an Old Testament Scripture, it is often prefaced by *"God says,"* or the *"Holy Spirit says."* The writer is reminding us that God is speaking to us through the Holy Scriptures. Our first task is to pay attention to the Word of God and hear what God is saying to us, with open hearts.

The Scripture selection is three chapters. Take turns by having each person read a paragraph or two aloud. As others are reading, be as attentive and present as possible to hear what the Lord is saying to you personally.

READ HEBREWS 1:1-3:19. (7-10 MINUTES)

WHAT DID YOU JUST HEAR THE WORD SAY TO YOU? (10-15 MINUTES)

3. Hebrews 1:1-2a says, "Long ago, at many times and in many ways, God spoke to our fathers by the prophets, but in these last days he has spoken to us by his Son...." How does this verse introduce the rest of chapters 1-3?

4. How are the Old and New Covenants being compared throughout these chapters?

5. What is the preacher's main concern for those who are hearing (reading) this? What response does the writer want the hearers to have?

Study Notes

DRAW NEAR TO THE THRONE

As we hear God's Word together, we are called to respond by being drawn into communion with God and community with one another.

6. How would you describe your typical experience with the ministry of the Word of God during the worship service?

7. What does the message of the "great salvation" offered through Jesus Christ mean to you personally? Briefly share your testimony of how he has saved you personally.

RUN THE RACE SET BEFORE YOU

The writer of Hebrews describes the life of a believer as a test of enduring faith. We are called to keep our eyes fixed on Jesus as we set out to be faithful to him.

8. What is your attitude this week toward worship of the Lord? What hinders you from deeply engaging in regular weekly worship of the Lord (the culture, temptation, trials, or difficulties with the church, etc.)?

9. Take care of your heart. Re-read Hebrews 3:12-14. Today, do you feel that your heart toward the Living God is hopeful and confident or hard and withdrawn? What causes hardness of heart toward God in your life? What helps inspire confident hope?

10. What proactive step of faith will you take today to be more attentive to the Word of the Living God?

11. How will you combat your own hardness of heart in the worship service itself this coming weekend?

12. Each day this week, you are provided a daily devotion where you can reflect more deeply on the Scriptures and spend time alone in prayer. Will you make a commitment to engage in this deeper study this week?

13. How can the group be praying for you? There is a place to write prayer requests on page ???

CLOSE IN PRAYER

O God, who wonderfully created, and yet more wonderfully restored, the dignity of human nature: Grant that we may share the divine life of him who humbled himself to share our humanity, your Son Jesus Christ; who lives and reigns with you, in the unity of the Holy Spirit, one God, for ever and ever. Amen.
—BCP, P. 214

DAILY DEVOTION

Studying the book of Hebrews is like mining a rich vein of gold. The deeper you dig, the more treasure you will discover. Spend time daily with the Lord. Each devotion will give you a brief portion of Scripture to read and a short meditation to stimulate your personal interaction with God and his Word. Pray and ask the Lord to reveal himself to you in your daily devotional time. Use the space provided to journal what you are hearing from the Lord or to express your petitions, thanksgivings, and praises to the Lord in prayer.

2

ENTERING FEARLESSLY INTO SABBATH REST

KEY VERSE

So then, there remains a Sabbath rest for the people of God, for whoever has entered God's rest has also rested from his works as God did from his. Let us therefore strive to enter that rest, so that no one may fall by the same sort of disobedience. — HEBREWS 4:9-11

SESSION INTRODUCTION:

The first chapter of Genesis is the paradigm for the entire narrative of human history. God is leading us out of Chaos into Sabbath Rest. The Israelites crossing the Jordan left the chaos of the wilderness to enter the Promised Land. They saw this journey as fulfillment of the promised Sabbath Rest.

And yet, the New Covenant holds out a greater promise of ultimate Sabbath Rest— full communion with the Living God. The preacher of Hebrews calls us to enter fully and wholeheartedly into that greater Sabbath Rest. Today is the day of commitment. It comes down to obedience.

Jesus learned obedience through sufferings and so was perfected as our Great High Priest. In this way, he alone can help us to fulfill our eternal calling. He is the source of eternal salvation to all who obey him.

Because of the challenges of this life, the temptation is to shrink back from the sovereign summons of God's Word. But to do so would be to fall away from salvation itself. It is not possible to go back to a pre-baptized, unconverted way of life. No, there is only one way for the people of God who have crossed the Jordan River of baptism to go, and that is forward.

Go deeper; draw closer into faithful relational intimacy with the Living God. There is no turning back from communion with God once you have made that commitment to him.

Opening Prayer

USE THIS PRAYER OR PRAY ONE OF YOUR OWN. YOU MAY WANT TO SAY IT TOGETHER.

O Almighty God, who pours out on all who desire it the spirit of grace and of supplication: Deliver us, when we draw near to you, from coldness of heart and wanderings of mind, that with steadfast thoughts and kindled affections we may worship you in spirit and in truth; through Jesus Christ our Lord. Amen.

—BCP p. 833

GETTING STARTED

1. Where do you go to find peace?

2. Is Sabbath Rest something that is important to you? What does the idea of Sabbath Rest mean to you?

WATCH THE VIDEO / SESSION 2
https://biblestudymedia.com/drawnear/

Pay Attention to the Word

The Word of God is *"living and active"* (4:12). Our first task is to pay attention to the Word of God and hear what God is saying to us with open hearts.

The Scripture selection is several chapters. Take turns by having each person read a paragraph or two aloud. As others are reading, be as attentive and present as possible to hear what the Lord is saying to you personally.

READ HEBREWS 4:1-6:12 (6-9 MINUTES)

WHAT DID YOU JUST HEAR THE WORD SAY TO YOU? (10−15 MINUTES)

3. How is the term "Sabbath Rest" being used in these chapters?

4. Why did the people of God in Joshua's day fail to enter the Rest of God? (See 4:2,6.) Do you see the same issues in our day? If so, in what ways?

5. How does Jesus become for us the source of eternal salvation (5:9)? What is eternal salvation?

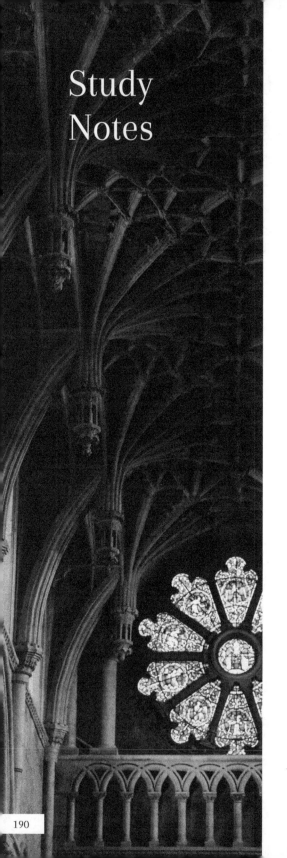

Study Notes

DRAW NEAR TO THE THRONE

As we hear God's Word together, we are called to respond by being drawn into communion with God and community with one another.

6. Honestly evaluate your own spiritual maturity—do you still need milk or are you ready for solid food?

7. What do you think it means to "go on toward maturity"? (See 5:11-6:3.) Is there anything preventing you from doing that?

8. What are some of the examples of spiritual maturity that the preacher names? (See 5:12, 6:10.) How do you see these examples manifest in your own life? In the other

members of your study group?

RUN THE RACE SET BEFORE YOU

The writer of Hebrews describes the life of a believer as a test of enduring faith. We are called to keep our eyes fixed on Jesus as we set out to be faithful to him.

9. Hebrews 5:12 says that "by this time you ought to be teachers." What would it take to get you to the point of becoming a teacher of the basics of the Christian faith to others? What practical steps will you commit to take in this direction?

10. In the name of Jesus, what good work or act of love can you show to the saints of God this week?

11. What causes you to be "sluggish" in your spiritual growth? Where do you need to be more faithful with the Lord this week?

12. Each day this week, you are provided a daily devotion where you can reflect more deeply on the Scriptures and spend time alone in prayer. Will you make a commitment to engage in this deeper study this week?

13. How can the group be praying for you? There is a place to write prayer requests on page ???.

CLOSE IN PRAYER

Almighty God, who after the creation of the world rested from all your works and sanctified a day of rest for all your creatures: Grant that we, putting away all earthly anxieties, may be duly prepared for the service of your sanctuary, and that our rest here upon earth may be a preparation for the eternal rest promised to your people in heaven; through Jesus Christ our Lord. Amen. —BCP P. 99

DAILY DEVOTION

Studying the book of Hebrews is like mining a rich vein of gold. The deeper you dig, the more treasure you will discover. Spend time daily with the Lord. Each devotion will give you a brief portion of Scripture to read and a short meditation to stimulate your personal interaction with God and his Word. Pray and ask the Lord to reveal himself to you in your daily devotional time. Use the space provided to journal what you are hearing from the Lord or to express your petitions, thanksgivings, and praises to the Lord in prayer.

3

MEETING OUR GREAT HIGH PRIEST

KEY VERSE

We have this as a sure and steadfast anchor of the soul, a hope that enters into the inner place behind the curtain, where Jesus has gone as a forerunner on our behalf, having become a high priest forever after the order of Melchizedek. — HEBREWS 6:19-20

SESSION

INTRODUCTION:

One of the reasons we can become disillusioned with the church is because of the frail and finite people leading the church. Discouragement and hurt can move us out of regular worship of the Lord.

But we must learn that our access to God is first and foremost through Jesus, who is our Great High Priest. He alone is the one who can, and rightfully ought to, lead the people of God into the presence of God. He will never disappoint. We can place our full confidence and hope in him. Our great salvation is guaranteed by the oath and covenant of God and by the eternal ministry of our Great High Priest.

There are two priestly orders in the Bible. One priesthood is earthly and temporal, the Levitical priesthood in the Order of Aaron and Levi. The preacher of Hebrews argues that the greater priesthood is in the Order of Melchizedek—this priesthood is eternal and permanent. Jesus is the Great High Priest in the Order of Melchizedek. We read about Melchizedek in Genesis 14:

> And Melchizedek king of Salem brought out bread and wine. (He was priest of God Most High.) And he blessed [Abram] and said, "Blessed be Abram by God Most High, Possessor of heaven and earth; and blessed be God Most High, who has delivered your enemies into your hand!" And Abram gave him a tenth of everything.   —Genesis 14:18-20

Melchizedek's priesthood is royal. In the same way, Jesus is both our King and our Priest. The Lord has promised, by oath, that Jesus alone will bring us to himself. The sanctuary, the sacrifices, and the priesthood of Melchizedek are of a higher order of which the earthly and temporal tabernacle, sacrifices, and priesthood of Aaron and Levi were but shadows and copies.

In our worship, as people of the New Covenant, we must learn to trust our hearts less to those leading our service of worship and more to the leading and ministry of our Great High Priest, Jesus. We find our confidence and hope in him.

Opening Prayer

USE THIS PRAYER OR PRAY ONE OF YOUR
OWN. YOU MAY WANT TO SAY IT TOGETHER.

*Grant us, Lord, not to be anxious about earthly things, but to
love things heavenly; and even now, while we are placed among
things that are passing away, to hold fast to those that shall
endure; through Jesus Christ our Lord, who lives and reigns
with you and the Holy Spirit, one God, for ever and ever. Amen.*

—BCP, p. 234

GETTING STARTED

1. Who is the most trustworthy leader in your life?

2. What do you hope to experience when you come
   to church to worship?

WATCH THE VIDEO / SESSION 3
https://biblestudymedia.com/drawnear/

DRAW NEAR

HEBREWS
ON CHRISTIAN
WORSHIP

THE REV.
CHARLIE
HOLT

Pay Attention to the Word

When the book of Hebrews quotes an Old Testament Scripture, it is often prefaced by *"God says,"* or the *"Holy Spirit says."* The writer is reminding us that God is speaking to us through the Holy Scriptures. Our first task is to pay attention to the Word of God and hear what God is saying to us, with open hearts.

The Scripture selection is several chapters long. Take turns by having each person read a paragraph or two aloud. As others are reading, be as attentive and present as possible to hear what the Lord is saying to you personally.

READ HEBREWS 6:13-8:13. (7-10 MINUTES)

WHAT DID YOU JUST HEAR THE WORD SAY TO YOU? (10-15 MINUTES)

3. What do you think it means to enter "the inner place behind the curtain" (6:19)?

4. What are the problems and limitations with the earthly ministers of God represented by the Levitical priesthood? (See 7:23, 27, 28.) Why is the Melchizedekian priesthood superior?

5. How is Jesus' priesthood and ministry different from that of the Levites?

6. Why is the new covenant better than the old? (See 8:6-13.)

Study Notes

DRAW NEAR TO THE THRONE

As we hear God's Word together, we are called to respond by being drawn into communion with God and community with one another.

7. Is church a safe place for you to feel vulnerable before God? Why or why not?

8. Have you ever been disappointed with or let down by a spiritual leader? If so, how did that affect your relationship to God within the worship life of the Church?

9. Have you ever visualized that Jesus is guiding and directing the worship of your church service? If so, what helps you to see Jesus as leading you in weekly worship? What hinders you from seeing him?

10. Read this promise of God concerning the New Covenant:

I will put my laws into their minds, and write them on their hearts, and I will be their God, and they shall be my people.

And they shall not teach, each one his neighbor and each one his brother, saying, "Know the Lord," for they shall all know me, from the least of them to the greatest.

For I will be merciful toward their iniquities, and I will remember their sins no more.
—Hebrews 8:10b-12

How trustworthy is this promise of God to you? What part of this promise is most significant to you?

RUN THE RACE SET BEFORE YOU

The writer of Hebrews describes the life of a believer as a test of enduring faith. We are called to keep our eyes fixed on Jesus as we set out to be faithful to him.

11. Abraham is said to have paid tithes (a tenth part of everything) to "*the one of whom it is testified that he lives*" (7:8). How does the spiritual discipline of tithing (giving a tenth of your income to the Lord) tangibly represent your complete trust in Jesus, the King of Righteousness and Peace? How does your giving reflect your heart?

12. As the priest who "*continues forever,*" Jesus "*lives to make intercession*" for his people (7:25). What prayers of intercession will you offer up to the Great High Priest today? Spend the remainder of your time together offering your intercessions to the Lord.

CLOSE IN PRAYER

O Lord our God, accept the fervent prayers of your people; in the multitude of your mercies, look with compassion upon us and all who turn to you for help; for you are gracious, O lover of souls, and to you we give glory, Father, Son, and Holy Spirit, now and for ever. Amen. —BCP, P. 395.

DAILY DEVOTION

Studying the book of Hebrews is like mining a rich vein of gold. The deeper you dig, the more treasure you will discover. Spend time daily with the Lord. Each devotion will give you a brief portion of Scripture to read and a short meditation to stimulate your personal interaction with God and his Word. Pray and ask the Lord to reveal himself to you in your daily devotional time. Use the space provided to journal what you are hearing from the Lord or to express your petitions, thanksgivings, and praises to the Lord in prayer.

4

DRAWING NEAR TO THE MOST HOLY PLACE

Therefore, brothers, since we have confidence to enter the holy places by the blood of Jesus, by the new and living way that he opened for us through the curtain, that is, through his flesh, and since we have a great priest over the house of God, let us draw near with a true heart in full assurance of faith, with our hearts sprinkled clean from an evil conscience and our bodies washed with pure water. — HEBREWS 10:19-22

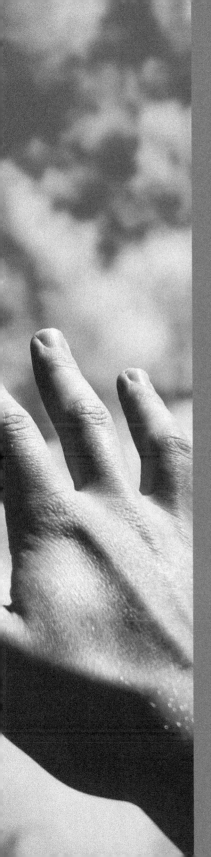

SESSION INTRODUCTION:

In the Old Covenant, the people of God approached the throne of God through the mediation of the Tabernacle of the Lord. The Ark of the Covenant, within the Most Holy Place of the Tabernacle, was considered to be the footstool of the throne of God. The Holy Place and the Holy of Holies were the two inner chambers of the Tabernacle. These two chambers were inaccessible to the common person. Only the Priests could enter the Holy Place, and only the High Priest could enter the Holy of Holies. A curtain-like veil blocked access for any other individual.

God has been very particular about the way in which he is to be approached in worship. In the Old Covenant, he had strict and particular regulations about the worshiper's approach to him. The priest gave blood sacrifices to atone of his own sins and the sins of the people. But these were mere earthly copies of heavenly worship. These sacrifices were never adequate or sufficient to grant us full communion with the Lord.

With New Covenant worship, there is also a correct way into the throne room of grace. It also requires priestly mediation and a blood sacrifice for sin. The difference is, Jesus, our Great

High Priest, has offered *himself* as the atoning sacrifice for our sins, once for all. Because of Jesus' sacrifice, and through him, we can now enter the Holy of Holies—into the very presence of the Living God—through a new and living way. Jesus is that way.

Because of Jesus' atoning death for us, we are forgiven, by grace. This grace also cleanses and purifies us, giving us Jesus' perfect righteousness. The Lord gave us a tangible means to experience this perfecting grace in the Lord's Supper, or Holy Communion. The Gospel of Luke records Jesus' words of institution: *"And he took bread, and when he had given thanks, he broke it and gave it to them, saying, 'This is my body, which is given for you. Do this in remembrance of me.' And likewise, the cup after they had eaten, saying, 'This cup that is poured out for you is the new covenant in my blood'"* (Luke 22:19-20).

By faith, we "eat" Jesus' flesh and "drink" his blood. *"Jesus said, 'I am the bread of life; whoever comes to me shall not hunger, and whoever believes in me shall never thirst'"* (John 6:35). This is why Jesus instituted the Holy Communion: he did not want us to forget the very heart of our great salvation, in and through him.

Opening Prayer

USE THIS PRAYER OR PRAY ONE OF YOUR OWN. YOU MAY WANT TO SAY IT TOGETHER.

Almighty God, you have given your only Son to be for us a sacrifice for sin, and also an example of godly life: Give us grace to receive thankfully the fruits of this redeeming work, and to follow daily in the blessed steps of his most holy life; through Jesus Christ your Son our Lord, who lives and reigns with you and the Holy Spirit, one God, now and for ever. Amen.

–BCP, p 232.

GETTING STARTED

1. When are the times that you feel closest to God?

2. A sacrament is an outward and visible sign of an inward and spiritual grace. What is the outward and visible sign and what is the inward grace in the sacrament of Holy Communion?

WATCH THE VIDEO / SESSION 4
https://biblestudymedia.com/drawnear/

Pay Attention to the Word

When the book of Hebrews quotes an Old Testament Scripture, it is often prefaced by *"God says,"* or the *"Holy Spirit says."* The writer is reminding us that God is speaking to us through the Holy Scriptures. Our first task is to pay attention to the Word of God and hear what God is saying to us, with open hearts.

The Scripture selection is two chapters long. Take turns by having each person read a paragraph or two aloud. As others are reading, be as attentive and present as possible to hear what the Lord is saying to you personally.

READ HEBREWS 9:1-10:31. (5-7 MINUTES)

WHAT DID YOU JUST HEAR THE WORD SAY TO YOU? (10-15 MINUTES)

3. What was required in the Old Covenant to approach the Holy of Holies? Who could enter and when?

4. Why is blood sacrifice necessary for access to the throne room of God?

5. What are the limitations of the Old Covenant blood sacrifices?

6. How does Jesus' sacrifice become the superior sacrifice for sin?

Study Notes

DRAW NEAR TO THE THRONE

As we hear God's Word together, we are called to respond by being drawn into communion with God and community with one another.

7. What do you think the Word of God means when it says, "we have confidence to enter the holy places by the blood of Jesus, by the new and living way that he opened for us through the curtain, that is, through his flesh" (10:19-20)? How do these words inform our experience with Holy Communion?

8. Have you ever thought of the approach to the Lord's Table as entering the Holy of Holies? What does Holy Communion mean to you personally?

9. We read in John 6:53-55:

"So Jesus said to them, 'Truly, truly, I say to you, unless you eat the flesh of the Son of Man and

drink his blood, you have no life in you. Whoever feeds on my flesh and drinks my blood has eternal life, and I will raise him up on the last day. For my flesh is true food, and my blood is true drink.'"

In what manner are we to eat Jesus' flesh and drink Jesus' blood? (See Hebrews 10:22.)

RUN THE RACE SET BEFORE YOU

The writer of Hebrews describes the life of a believer as a test of enduring faith. We are called to keep our eyes fixed on Jesus as we set out to be faithful to him.

10. The preacher encourages us to "not [neglect] to meet together, as is the habit of some" (10:25). Why do some believers get out of the habit of regular fellowship with the church? Why is it so important to gather together often?

11. What is encouragement? How can Christians encourage one another? Why do we need it? Try offering a genuine encouragement to each person in your group.

12. Think of some practical ways that we could "stir up one another to love and good works" (10:24)? Perhaps the Lord would place on your hearts some love and good works that you could do together as a group.

13. The preacher of Hebrews strongly discourages "sinning deliberately after receiving the knowledge of the truth" (10:26). Why would continuing in sin deliberately be so destructive? (Read 10:26-31.) In our modern culture, how do we take the grace of God for granted by treating our sin too lightly?

14. Share any prayer requests and spend the remainder of your time together offering your intercessions to the Lord for one another.

CLOSE IN PRAYER

Most holy God, the source of all good desires, all right judgements, and all just works: Give to us, your servants, that peace which the world cannot give, so that our minds may be fixed on the doing of your will, and that we, being delivered from the fear of all enemies, may live in peace and quietness; through the mercies of Christ Jesus our Savior. Amen. —BCP P. 123

DAILY DEVOTION

Studying the book of Hebrews is like mining a rich vein of gold. The deeper you dig, the more treasure you will discover. Spend time daily with the Lord. Each devotion will give you a brief portion of Scripture to read and a short meditation to stimulate your personal interaction with God and his Word. Pray and ask the Lord to reveal himself to you in your daily devotional time. Use the space provided to journal what you are hearing from the Lord or to express your petitions, thanksgivings, and praises to the Lord in prayer.

5

TRUSTING IN THINGS PROMISED YET UNSEEN

KEY VERSE

Therefore, since we are surrounded by so great a cloud of witnesses, let us also lay aside every weight, and sin which clings so closely, and let us run with endurance the race that is set before us, looking to Jesus, the founder and perfecter of our faith, who for the joy that was set before him endured the cross, despising the shame, and is seated at the right hand of the throne of God. — HEBREWS 12:1-2

SESSION INTRODUCTION:

Faith is a key antidote to cure what is ailing the church. When Christians are beginning to shrink back from intimacy with the Lord, their bold public confession and faith commitment to worship with one another is key. For an entire chapter, the preacher of Hebrews provides example after example of people of God who faced similar or greater challenges than the Church today and yet stood fast and maintained their faith in God. This section is often called "The Great Hall of Faith," "Faith Hall-of-Famers," or the "Litany of the Faithful."

The early Church Fathers speak of three types of faith in God:

- **Credere Deum** ("to believe that God is"): This is simply to believe that God exists. But this faith contains no moral assent. James says that even the demons believe in God, and they shudder (James 2:19).

- **Credere Deo** ("to believe toward God"): This is a faith that assents to the moral superiority of God and the trustworthiness of his Word. If God says of Jesus, *"This is my Son, listen to him,"* this type of faith believes it. If the promises say that Christ died for our sins to forgive us, a person with this faith believes that His word of promise is true and trustworthy.

- **Credere in Deum** (in Latin, literally: "to believe *into* God"): This is more difficult to translate, but it is a total reliance upon God, wherein a person literally rests in God. This is placing faith, trust—even yourself—*into* God. This is the highest expression of faith.

The preacher is encouraging his hearers to all three levels of faith. In fact, it is impossible to be approved by God and credited as righteous without all three.

And without faith it is impossible to please God, for whoever would approach him must believe that he exists and that he rewards those who seek him. —Hebrews 11:6

We must "*believe that he exists.*" *Credere Deum*: belief that God is. This is the way that God revealed himself to Moses in the name YHWH, "I am that I am" (Exodus 3:14, KJV). God is the God who is. As the preacher argues in the first chapter of Hebrews, this is the basic assumption of the Christian. God is there.

When polled, the vast majority of Americans (usually around 90%) affirm this type of faith in God. [1] But James warns that this type of faith is not enough—even devils have this kind of faith. It is not a faith that will save you. It is essential to believe that God is, yet this belief alone is insufficient.

Saving faith not only believes that God is, but it also believes that God's promises are good and true. As argued in Hebrews 1, God has continually revealed himself in various ways at various times. But in these last days, God has spoken definitively and supremely through his Son. God doesn't just exist, he also speaks to us, and he makes promises and covenants. Christian faith is a belief that God "*rewards those who seek him*" (11:6). His promises are true and trustworthy. We are called, then, to also believe toward God (*credere Deo*), to submit to his revelation and trust it.

While believing that God is and believing toward God are essential, the writer of Hebrews urges us toward the third and highest form of faith—credere in Deum, believing into God. He commends to us the heroes of the faith for exhibiting this third level of faith: entrusting their very lives to God, relying on the promises of God, and doing great things for God, even to the point of suffering and martyrdom.

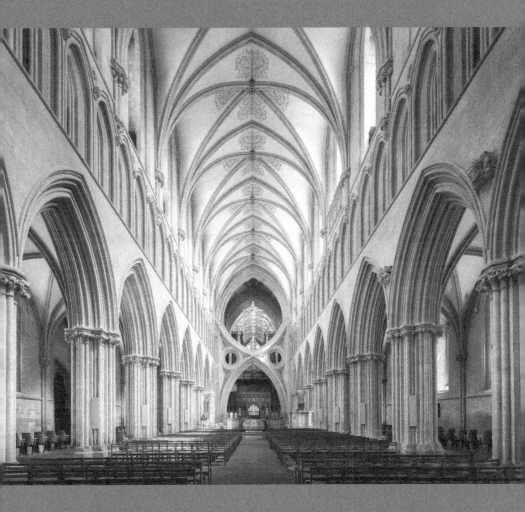

[1] http://www.gallup.com/poll/147887/Americans-Continue-Be-lieve-God.aspx

Opening Prayer

O God, who wonderfully created, and yet more wonderfully restored, the dignity of human nature: Grant that we may share the divine life of him who humbled himself to share our humanity, your Son Jesus Christ; who lives and reigns with you, in the unity of the Holy Spirit, one God, for ever and ever. Amen.

— BCP p. 252

GETTING STARTED

1. Of the three types of faith mentioned in the introduction, which type best describes your faith right now?

2. When someone says that they need "more faith," what might they mean?

WATCH THE VIDEO / SESSION 5
https://biblestudymedia.com/drawnear/

Pay Attention to the Word

When the book of Hebrews quotes an Old Testament Scripture, it is often prefaced by *"God says,"* or the *"Holy Spirit says."* The writer is reminding us that God is speaking to us through the Holy Scriptures. They are *"living and active"* (4:12). Our first task is to pay attention to the Word of God and hear what God is saying to us, with open hearts.

The Scripture selection is two chapters long. Take turns by having each person read a paragraph or two aloud. As others are reading, be as attentive and present as possible to hear what the Lord is saying to you personally.

READ HEBREWS 10:32-12:13. (5-7 MINUTES)

WHAT DID YOU JUST HEAR THE WORD SAY TO YOU? (10-15 MINUTES)

3. What are some of the *"hard struggles with suffering"* that were facing the original hearers of the sermon to the Hebrews (10:32-34)? How could these challenges have negatively affected their relationship to the Christian life? What did they need to do?

4. Where do you see examples of the three different types of faith (from the section introduction) described in Hebrews 11?

5. "By faith" is a key phrase in Hebrews 11. Hebrews 11:2 says, *"For by [faith] people of old received their commendation."* List some of the things the people of old did "by faith" and the commendation they received? What did they not receive (11:10-12, 16, 26, 35, 39-40)?

Study Notes

DRAW NEAR TO THE THRONE

As we hear God's Word together, we are called to respond by being drawn into communion with God and community with one another.

6. The *"great cloud of witnesses"* (12:1) encourages us, like cheering fans in a grandstand, to run the race of faith. But they are no mere spectators; they are runners who have already finished their race! What is the faith race that is set before you personally? How does Hebrews 12:1-2 inspire you?

7. Do you ever grow *"weary"* or *"fainthearted"* (12:3) in your Christian life? Where do you find encouragement to keep going?

8. Can you share the testimony of a *"painful discipline"* and how God used it to produce holiness and the *"peaceful fruit of righteousness"* in your Christian life (12:10-11)?

RUN THE RACE SET BEFORE YOU

9. Re-read Hebrews 12:12-13. This week, we are called to seek the Lord's healing of the lame and out-of-joint places in our Christian life:

"Lift your drooping hands" – Where are the places in which you need to get back to the service of the Lord in his church or in mission to the world? What is the first action you need to do to lift your hands to good work?

"Strengthen your weak knees" – Are there situations you are facing right now where you lack Christian courage? Will you commit to stand firm in the Lord? What do you need?

"Make straight paths for your feet" – What tempting distractions or discouraging detours are taking you off course from your Christian walk? How will you get back on track this week?

10. Pray for one another's sanctification and support in the areas you've just discussed.

11. Have a discussion as to what the group may want to study next. Perhaps you want to divide and multiply. Or, you may want to keep meeting as a group and do another study together.

CLOSE IN PRAYER

O God, you declare your almighty power chiefly in showing mercy and pity: Grant us the fullness of your grace, that we, running to obtain your promises, may become partakers of your heavenly treasure; through Jesus Christ our Lord, who lives and reigns with you and the Holy Spirit, one God, for ever and ever. Amen.
—BCP P. 234

DAILY DEVOTION

Studying the book of Hebrews is like mining a rich vein of gold. The deeper you dig, the more treasure you will discover. Spend time daily with the Lord. Each devotion will give you a brief portion of Scripture to read and a short meditation to stimulate your personal interaction with God and his Word. Pray and ask the Lord to reveal himself to you in your daily devotional time. Use the space provided to journal what you are hearing from the Lord or to express your petitions, thanksgivings, and praises to the Lord in prayer.

6

LIVING A LIFE OF ACCEPTABLE WORSHIP

KEY VERSE

But you have come to Mount Zion and to the city of the Living God, the heavenly Jerusalem, and to innumerable angels in festal gathering, and to the assembly of the firstborn who are enrolled in heaven, and to God, the judge of all, and to the spirits of the righteous made perfect, and to Jesus, the mediator of a new covenant, and to the sprinkled blood that speaks a better word than the blood of Abel. — HEBREWS 12:22-24

For 40 years, the nation of Israel wandered in the Sinai wilderness between Egypt and the Promised Land. They had very specific instructions as to how to set up camp, live in community, and associate with those outside the community. Their camp took a specific shape when it was set up correctly—a cruciform.

What a sight to stand on a high place and gaze upon the vista of the tents of Israel! Balaam said of the Israelite camps:

"How beautiful are your tents, O Jacob, your dwelling places, O Israel!" Numbers 24:5, NIV

Throughout the book of Hebrews, the preacher has primarily been focused on our interaction with God through worship, using the metaphor and imagery of the Old Covenant people of God who made camp in the desert on the way to the Promised Land. Their instructions for worship and for community life in the camp were given on Mount Sinai as the Lord spoke to Moses from the unapproachable mountain.

With the advent of Jesus, human beings are now offered direct access to the Living God in a new way of personal relationship with him. The instructions for us have not come from an unapproachable mountain, but directly from the Heavenly Jerusalem, the city of the Living God. The tent of meeting with its inner sanctuary, its priesthood, and sacrifices was a shadow and symbol of the Great Salvation offered through the Great High Priest, by the sacrifice of himself, once offered. We now have access to the heavenly sanctuary by faith, a new and living way.

The book of Hebrews not only teaches us the way to live in connected, intimate fellowship with God—it also implores us to realize that our very life depends on it. As the preacher says, "… *our God is a consuming fire*" (Hebrews 12:29). When we realize the awesome power of God, we are humbled by his offer of love, forgiveness, and restored relationship with us.

And embracing a restored relationship with God will manifest in restored relationships with other believers. Just as the shape of the Israelites' camp took a cruciform shape, with the tabernacle for meeting the Living God at the center of community life, so too will the shape of our relationships be patterned after the Cross with worship in the heavenly temple of the Living God central.

The final thoughts of the preacher turn toward answering the question, "How shall we then live" in light of our faith-filled worship of the Living God? What is the practical application of that Holy relationship with the Living God who dwells in the camp of his people? He has two primary concerns:

> How to live relationally *inside* the camp as God's holy chosen people.

> How to live *outside* the camp as those who, in unity with Christ, bear his reproach.

In both cases, we are to see our lives as united with the sacrifice of the Son of God, who lived in righteousness and holiness in every relationship.

Opening Prayer

USE THIS PRAYER OR PRAY ONE OF YOUR
OWN. YOU MAY WANT TO SAY IT TOGETHER.

*Almighty God, whose Son our Savior Jesus Christ is the light
of the world: Grant that your people, illumined by your Word
and Sacraments, may shine with the radiance of Christ's
glory, that he may be known, worshiped, and obeyed to the
ends of the earth; through Jesus Christ our Lord, who with
you and the Holy Spirit lives and reigns, one God, now and
for ever. Amen.*

— BCP, p. 215

GETTING STARTED

1. Do you feel like it is hard to live the Christian life authentically in
   our day and age? Why or why not?

2. What gives you courage when you feel like you
   are being "criticized" for your Christian faith
   or godly life choices?

WATCH THE VIDEO / SESSION 6
https://biblestudymedia.com/drawnear/

DRAW NEAR

HEBREWS
ON CHRISTIAN
WORSHIP

THE REV.
CHARLIE
HOLT

Pay Attention to the Word

When the book of Hebrews quotes an Old Testament Scripture, it is often prefaced by *"God says,"* or the *"Holy Spirit says."* The writer is reminding us that God is speaking to us through the Holy Scriptures. Our first task is to pay attention to the Word of God and hear what God is saying to us, with open hearts.

The Scripture selection is two chapters long. Take turns by having each person read a paragraph or two aloud. As others are reading, be as attentive and present as possible to hear what the Lord is saying to you personally.

READ HEBREWS 12:14-13:25. (6-8 MINUTES)

WHAT DID YOU JUST HEAR THE WORD SAY TO YOU? (10-15 MINUTES)

3. What does the warning mean: "See to it that none of you fail to obtain the grace of God" (12:15)? How does the story of Esau illustrate what that warning means? (See Genesis 25:29-34.)

4. What are ways that we choose to sell our birthright for a single meal? How does bitterness and sexual immorality fit into that (12:15-17)?

5. Compare the two mountains described in Hebrews 12:18-22 and the response of the people of God in both cases. What should our response be (12:23-29)?

6. What is the difference between the word the sprinkled blood of Jesus our Great High Priest speaks to us (12:24) compared to the cry of the blood of Abel? (See Genesis 4:10.) Why does one "speak a better word" than the other? What makes it better?

Study
Notes

DRAW NEAR TO THE THRONE

As we hear God's Word together, we are called to respond by being drawn into communion with God and community with one another.

7. How is Hebrews 12:22-24 a description of the church in assembled worship? Are you aware of this present reality when you gather in congregational worship? What would help you to become more aware of our connection to the *"city of the Living God"*? (See Hebrews 11:1.)

8. Where in your life have you put your trust in things that will be "shaken" and "removed?" How will you address that in light of this word from the Living God (12:25-29)?

9. Reread aloud Hebrews 12:28-29. Having studied the entire book of Hebrews, what do you think the preacher means by his concluding challenge: "*[Let] us offer to God acceptable worship*" ?

RUN THE RACE SET BEFORE YOU

The writer of Hebrews describes the life of a believer as a test of enduring faith. We are called to keep our eyes fixed on Jesus as we set out to be faithful to him both within the community of the faithful and outside the church in the world. Every day is a call to worship the Living God! Our faith will practically translate into loving fellowship and holiness of life within the camp of God and faithful witness of endurance as we bear the cross of Jesus outside the camp.

10. How can you practically show brotherly love this week to those who come into our fellowship⸺the stranger (13:1-2)? How has this group shown you brotherly love? How can you show love to those who can't come into our fellowship, those who are estranged and those imprisoned (13:3)?

11. Two places where Christians can lose a commitment to holiness are sexual morality and money matters. Do you feel that marriage is "*held in honor among all*" (13:4)? How does our culture work against being "*content with what you have*" (13:5)?

12. In what ways are you called to go with Jesus "*outside the camp and bear the reproach he endured*" (13:13)? How can this Christian community support you in your witness this week?

13. What has been the most meaningful lesson you have learned from this study?

14. What is the next step for your group?

CLOSE IN PRAYER

Lord Jesus Christ, you stretched out your arms of love on the hard wood of the cross that everyone might come within the reach of your saving embrace: So clothe us in your Spirit that we, reaching forth our hands in love, may bring those who do not know you to the knowledge and love of you; for the honor of your Name. Amen. —BCP P. 101

DAILY DEVOTION

Studying the book of Hebrews is like mining a rich vein of gold. The deeper you dig, the more treasure you will discover. Spend time daily with the Lord. Each devotion will give you a brief portion of Scripture to read and a short meditation to stimulate your personal interaction with God and his Word. Pray and ask the Lord to reveal himself to you in your daily devotional time. Use the space provided to journal what you are hearing from the Lord or to express your petitions, thanksgivings, and praises to the Lord in prayer.

Appendices

GREAT RESOURCES TO HELP MAKE
YOUR SMALL GROUP EXPERIENCE
EVEN BETTER!

Frequently Asked Questions

What do we do on the first night of our group?

Have a party! A "get to know you" coffee, dinner, or dessert is a great way to launch a new study. You may want to review the Small Group Covenant (page 236) and share the names of a few friends you can invite to join you. But most importantly, have fun before your study time begins.

Where do we find new members for our group?

Finding members can be troubling, especially for new groups that have only a few people or for existing groups that lose a few people along the way. We encourage you to pray with your group and then brainstorm a list of people from work, church, your neighborhood, your children's school, family, the gym, and so forth. Use the five circles to identify potential group members with whom you would like to build a spiritual friendship. Have each group member invite several of the people on his or her list.

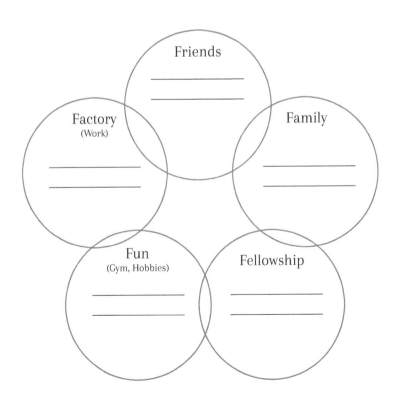

No matter how you find members, it's vital that you stay on the lookout for new people to join your group. All groups tend to go through healthy attrition—the result of moves, sending out new leaders, ministry opportunities, and so forth—and if the group gets too small, it could be at risk of ending. If you and your group stay open to ideas, you'll be amazed at the people God sends your way. The next person just might become a friend for life. You never know!

How long will this group meet?
Most groups meet weekly for at least their first 6 weeks, but every other week can work as well. We strongly recommend that the group meet for the first six months on a weekly basis if at all possible. This allows for continuity and, if people miss a meeting, they aren't gone for a whole month.

At the end of this study, each group member may decide if he or she wants to continue on for another 6-week study. Some groups launch relationships for years to come, and others are stepping-stones into another group experience. Either way, enjoy the journey.

Can we do this study on our own?
Absolutely! This may sound crazy, but one of the best ways to do this study is not with a full house but with a few friends. You may choose to gather with another couple who would enjoy some relational time (perhaps going to the movies or having a quiet dinner) and then walking through this 6-week study. Jesus will be with you even if there are only two of you (Matthew 18:20).

What if this group is not working for us?
You're not alone! This could be the result of a personality conflict, life stage difference, geographical distance, level of spiritual maturity, or any number of things. Relax. Pray for God's direction, and at the end of this 6-week study, decide whether to continue with this group or find another. You don't typically buy the first car you test drive or marry the first person you date, and the same goes with a group. However, don't bail out before the 6 weeks are up— God might have something to teach you. Also, don't run from conflict or prejudge people before you have given them a chance. God is still working in your life, too!

Who is the leader?

Most groups have an official leader. But ideally, the group will mature and members will rotate the leadership of meetings. We have discovered that healthy groups rotate hosts/leaders and homes on a regular basis. This model ensures that all members grow, make their unique contribution, and develop their gifts. This study guide and the Holy Spirit can keep things on track even when you rotate leaders. Christ has promised to be in your midst as you gather. Ultimately, God is your leader each step of the way.

How do we handle the childcare needs in our group?

Very carefully. This can be a sensitive issue. We suggest that you empower the group to openly brainstorm solutions. You may try one option that works for a while and then adjust over time. Our favorite approach is for adults to meet in the living room or dining room and to share the cost of a babysitter (or two) who can watch the children in a different part of the house. This way, parents don't have to be away from their children all evening when their children are too young to be left at home. A second option is to use one home for the children and a second home (close by or a phone call away) for the adults. A third idea is to rotate the responsibility of providing a lesson or care for the children either in the same home or in another home nearby. This can be an incredible blessing for young ones. Finally, the most common solution is to decide that you need to have a night to invest in your spiritual lives individually or as a couple and to make your own arrangements for childcare. No matter what decision the group makes, the best approach is to dialogue openly about both the need and the solution.

Small Group Covenant

Our Purpose
To provide a predictable environment where participants experience authentic Christian community to grow spiritually.

Group Attendance
To give priority to the group meeting. We will call or email if we will be late or absent. (Completing the Group Calendar on page 238 will minimize this issue.)

Safe Environment
To help create a safe place where people can be heard and feel loved. (Please, no quick answers, snap judgments, or simple fixes.)

Respect Differences
To be gentle and gracious with different spiritual maturity levels, personal opinions, temperaments, or "imperfections" in fellow group members. We are all works in progress.

Confidentiality
To keep anything that is shared strictly confidential and within the group, and to avoid sharing improper information about those outside the group.

Encouragement for Growth
To be not just takers, but givers of life. We want to spiritually multiply our lives by serving others with our God-given gifts.

Shared Ownership
To remember that every member is a minister and to ensure that each attender will share a small team role or responsibility over time.

Rotating Hosts/ Facilitators and Homes
To encourage different people to host the group in their homes and to rotate the responsibility of facilitating each meeting. (See the Group Calendar on page 238)

Our Expectations

Refreshments/mealtimes:

Childcare:

When we will meet (day of week):

Where we will meet (place):

We will begin at (time):   and end at:

We will do our best to have some or all of us attend a worship service together. Our primary worship service time will be:

Date of this agreement:

Date we will review this agreement again:

Who (other than the leader) will review this agreement at the end of this study:

Group Calendar

Planning and calendaring can help ensure the greatest participation
at every meeting. At the end of each meeting, review this calendar.
Be sure to include a regular rotation of host homes and facilitator,
and don't forget birthdays, socials, church events, holidays, and
mission/ministry projects.

Date	Session	Host Home	Snacks	Facilitator
	1			
	2			
	3			
	4			
	5			
	6			

Prayer and Praise Report

Session 1

Session 2

Session 3

Session 4

Session 5

Session 6

Small Group Roster

Use the chart below to collect names and contact information from all the group members. We suggest that one member (other than the host) "own" the task of collecting and distributing the contact info to everyone—via group text message or email—so that people can be in touch.

Name	Email	Cell Phone

Small Group Leader Helps

KEY RESOURCES TO HELP YOUR
LEADERSHIP EXPERIENCE BE THE
BEST IT CAN BE.

Hosting an Open House

If you're starting a new group, try planning an "open house" before your first formal group meeting. Even if you have only two to four core members, it's a great way to break the ice and to consider prayerfully who else might be open to joining you over the next few weeks. You can also use this kick-off meeting to hand out study guides, spend some time getting to know each other, discuss each person's expectations for the group and briefly pray for each other. A simple meal or good dessert always make a kick-off meeting more fun. After people introduce themselves and share how they ended up being at the meeting (you can play a game to see who has the wildest story!), have everyone respond to a few icebreaker questions, such as:

- What is your favorite family vacation?
- What is one thing you love about your church/our community?
- What are three things about your life growing up that most people here don't know?

Next, ask everyone to tell what he or she hopes to get out of the study. You might want to review the Small Group Covenant on page ??? and talk about each person's expectations and priorities. Finally, set an open chair (maybe two) in the center of your group and explain that it represents someone who would enjoy or benefit from this group but who isn't here yet.

Ask people to pray about inviting someone to join the group over the next few weeks. Hand out postcards and have everyone write an invitation or two. Don't worry about ending up with too many people; you can always have one discussion circle in the living room and another in the dining room after you watch the lesson. Each group could then report prayer requests and progress at the end of the session.

You can skip this kick-off meeting if your time is limited, but you'll experience a huge benefit if you take the time to connect with one another in this way.

Leading for the First Time

(Seven common leadership experiences. Welcome to life out in front!)

- **Sweaty palms are a healthy sign.** The Bible says God is gracious to the humble. Remember who is in control; the time to worry is when you're not worried. Those who are soft in heart (and sweaty palmed) are those whom God is sure to speak through.

- **Seek support.** Ask your leader, co-leader, or close friend to pray for you and prepare with you before the session. Walking through the study will help you anticipate potentially difficult questions and discussion topics.

- **Bring your uniqueness to the study.** Lean into who you are and how God wants you to uniquely lead the study.

- **Prepare. Prepare. Prepare.** Go through the session, read the section of Scripture. If you are using the Video, listen to the teaching segment. Consider writing in a journal or praying through the day to prepare yourself for what God wants to do. Don't wait until the last minute to prepare.

- **Ask for feedback so you can grow.** Perhaps in an email or on cards handed out at the study, have everyone write down three things you did well and one thing you could improve on. Don't get defensive. Instead, show an openness to learn and grow.

- **Share with your group what God is doing in your heart.** God is searching for those whose hearts are fully his. Share your trials and victories. We promise that people will relate.

- **Prayerfully consider whom you would like to pass the baton to next week.** It's only fair. God is ready for the next member of your group to go on the faith journey you just traveled. Make it fun, and expect God to do the rest.

Leadership Training 101

Congratulations! You have responded to the call to help shepherd Jesus' flock. There are few other tasks in the family of God that surpass the contribution you will be making. As you prepare to lead, whether it is one session or the entire series, here are a few thoughts to keep in mind. We encourage you to read these and review them with each new discussion leader before he or she leads.

1. Remember that you are not alone. God knows everything about you, and he knew that you would be asked to lead your group. Remember that it is common for all good leaders to feel that they are not ready to lead. Moses, Solomon, Jeremiah, and Timothy were all reluctant to lead. God promises, "Never will I leave you; never will I forsake you" (Hebrews 13:5). Whether you are leading for one evening, for several weeks, or for a lifetime, you will be blessed as you serve.

2. Don't try to do it alone. Pray right now for God to help you build a healthy leadership team. If you can enlist a co-leader to help you lead the group, you will find your experience to be much richer. This is your chance to involve as many people as you can in building a healthy group. All you have to do is call and ask people to help. You'll probably be surprised at the response.

3. Just be yourself. If you won't be you, who will? God wants you to use your unique gifts and temperament. Don't try to do things exactly like another leader; do them in a way that fits you! Just admit it when you don't have an answer, and apologize when you make a mistake. Your group will love you for it, and you'll sleep better at night!

4. Prepare for your meeting ahead of time. Review the session, and write down your responses to each question. Pay special attention to exercises that ask group members to do something other than engage in discussion. These exercises will help your group live what the Bible teaches, not just talk about it.

5. Pray for your group members by name. Before you begin your session, go around the room in your mind and pray for each member by name. You may want to review the prayer list at least once a week. Ask God to use your time together to touch the heart of every person uniquely. Expect God to lead you to whomever he wants you to encourage or challenge in a special way. If you listen, God will surely lead!

6. When you ask a question, be patient. Someone will eventually respond. Sometimes people need a moment or two of silence to think about the question. Keep in mind, if silence doesn't bother you, it won't bother anyone else. After someone responds, affirm the response with a simple "thanks" or "good job." Then ask, "How about somebody else?" or "Would someone who hasn't shared like to add anything?" Be sensitive to new people or reluctant members who aren't ready to say, pray, or do anything. If you give them a safe setting, they will blossom over time.

7. Provide transitions between questions. When guiding the discussion, always read aloud the transitional paragraphs and the questions. Ask the group if anyone would like to read the paragraph or Bible passage. Don't call on anyone, but ask for volunteers, and then be patient until someone begins. Be sure to thank the people who read aloud.

8. Break up into small groups each week or they won't stay. If your group has a lot of people, we strongly encourage you to have the group gather sometimes in discussion circles of three or four people during the Draw Near to the Throne or Run the Race Set Before You sections of the study. With a greater opportunity to talk in a small circle, people will connect more with the study, apply more quickly what they're learning, and ultimately get more out of it. A small circle also encourages a quiet person to participate and tends to minimize the effects of a more vocal or dominant member. It can also help people feel more loved in your group.

When you gather again at the end of the section, you can have one person summarize the highlights from each circle. Small circles are also helpful during prayer time. People who are unaccustomed to praying aloud will feel more comfortable trying it with just two or three others.

Also, prayer requests won't take as much time, so circles will have more time to actually pray. When you gather back with the whole group, you can have one person from each circle briefly update everyone on the prayer requests. People are more willing to pray in small circles if they know that the whole group will hear all the prayer requests.

9. Rotate facilitators weekly. At the end of each meeting, ask the group who should lead the following week. Let the group help select your weekly facilitator. You may be perfectly capable of leading each time, but you will help others grow in their faith and gifts if you give them opportunities to lead. You can use the Small Group Calendar to fill in the names of all meeting leaders at once if you prefer.

10. One final challenge (for new or first time leaders):
Before your first opportunity to lead, look up each of the five passages listed below. Read each one as a devotional exercise to help equip yourself with a shepherd's heart. Trust us on this one. If you do this, you will be more than ready for your first meeting.

Matthew 9:36
1 Peter 5:2-4
Psalm 23
Ezekiel 34:11-16
1 Thessalonians 2:7-8, 11-12

Now may the God of peace who brought
again from the dead our Lord Jesus,
the great shepherd of the sheep, by the
blood of the eternal covenant, equip
you with everything good that you may
do his will, working in us that which
is pleasing in his sight, through Jesus
Christ, to whom be glory forever and
ever. Amen.

HEBREWS 13:20-21

Donation

Bible Study Media's aim is to renew Christian communities with Gospel-centered, heart-changing curriculum.

OUR MISSION:

To foster lifelong biblical learning and an intimate relationship with Jesus Christ.

To bring believers together and strengthen the bonds of community. To produce engaging, faithful, and applicable Christian teaching resources for churches and individuals.

The development cost of our vital projects are being funded by the generous donations of people like you!

If you would like to discuss contributions to the development of our current projects and future Christian Formation resources visit **www.biblestudymedia.com.**

Acknowledgements

There are so many people who have helped make this study possible through generous donations of their time, passion, and participation. Thank you to all who have contributed to this project offered to the glory of God:

Brooke Holt
Todd Wilson
Sam Dunnaway
Doug McMurray
Walter Berring
Temple Webber
Cathy Brock
Mark Stamey
Ted Cooper
Susie Millonig
Jim Grisham
Karen Williams
Sarah McParland

Calvin Harris
Ross Adams
JC Al-Uqdah
Paige Poe
Dawayne Gaspard
Ginny Mooney
Mitch Jefferies
Marilyn Gore
Andrea Meyer
Tani James
Blueprint Films
Tommy Owen Design
The Churches of St. Peter's Episcopal Church, Lake Mary Florida and St. John the Divine, Houston Texas

DRAW NEAR

HEBREWS
ON CHRISTIAN
WORSHIP

CPSIA information can be obtained
at www.ICGtesting.com
Printed in the USA
BVHW052204130319
542611BV00008B/53/P